CORE VALUES:

Styles and Practices of Successful Military Leaders

by

Dr. Janice M. Brooks, Master Sergeant, USMC, Ret.

DORRANCE
PUBLISHING CO
EST. 1920
PITTSBURGH, PENNSYLVANIA 15208

Dorrance Publishing Co
585 Alpha Drive
Suite 103
Pittsburgh, PA 15238
Visit our website at *www.dorrancebookstore.com*

ISBN: 978-1-4809-4428-2
eISBN: 978-1-4809-4451-0

A Dissertation Presented in Partial Fulfillment
of the Requirements for the Degree
Doctor of Management in Organizational Leadership

UNIVERSITY OF PHOENIX
March 2011

Approved:

Diane Gavin, PhD, Mentor
Brenda Curry, Ed.D., Committee Member
Ann Deaton, PhD., Committee Member

Accepted and Signed: Diane Gavin   03/15/2011
Accepted and Signed: Brenda Curry 03/15/2011
Accepted and Signed: Ann Deaton   03/15/2011

Jeremy Moreland, PhD.
Dean, School of Advanced Studies
University of Phoenix 03/29/2011

ABSTRACT

World affairs in the 21st century and increased diversity in the nature of military missions have placed responsibilities on the U.S. military, demanding a strict military ethos and unparalleled leadership ethics. Although many personal attributes interact to determine the effectiveness of those in leadership roles, perhaps the most crucial determinant of behavior and effectiveness is values. The present study used a qualitative grounded theory approach to determine the values held by eight proven successful military leaders. A Holistic and Humanistic Values-based leadership model was created to describe the proclaimed leadership values. The model is expected to meet leadership training goals of developing a person-centered force committed to ethical values while accomplishing the unique missions of a 21st century military force.

DEDICATION

This work is dedicated to the loving memory of my wonderful parents, Elder Cornelius and Rosetta Jones. They were always the source of motivation and encouragement to me and my siblings in everything we endeavored to achieve. My parents successfully raised eight children, each achieving lifetime accomplishments in their own right. Because they were charitable and loving Christians, biblical principles always formed the bedrock of their teaching, training, and disciplining, and continue to influence the lifestyle and spirituality of not only their own children but also many others who had the privilege of knowing them. Although they both now rest with the Savior, the truths they taught us and the lifestyle they modeled have continued to be the source of guidance in the way each of us conducts our lives and raises our own children.

ACKNOWLEDGMENTS

First and foremost, I acknowledge and give thanks to my God and my Lord and Savior Jesus Christ for providing me with the ability, the desire, and the determination to undertake this work for his glory and his alone. Without God, I can do nothing (John 15:4-5), but in His strength, I can do all things (Philippians 4:13).

Many thanks to my husband, Carl M. Brooks, Sr., SgtMaj., USMC (Ret.), who unwaveringly provided the moral, emotional, and financial support along with the encouragement necessary, while he persevered with me through the completion of this long and arduous process. He also provided experiential and technical military knowledge and expertise for me when needed, and ensured I had the sufficient level of information technology required for this process always available to me at every juncture.

I must also acknowledge and thank my daughter, Khoe Wraelle Winchester; her husband, Deon Shelton Winchester; and my son, U.S. army Staff Sergeant Carl M. Brooks, Jr., for their loving support and encouragement all along the way. I would like to make special mention of someone very special to me: my granddaughter, four-year-old Jahzara Trinitee Elizabeth Winchester ("Chuka"), who endured countless hours of waiting patiently for Grammy to finish her "homework" so we could play, have tea parties, or go on walks together. Many, many thanks and blessings to my lovely granddaughter, Jahzara.

I must also thank each of my eight siblings for their prayers, support, and encouragement, which have meant so much to me and which have been sources of strength and motivation every step of the way. Special thanks to my sister Dr. Avis T. Jones-Petlane for the professional expertise, advice, experience, and knowledge she contributed to this effort.

I also acknowledge and am thankful to my spiritual family, Spirit Song Church, for their love and support. I am especially grateful to my pastors, Larry and Nadine Hernandez, who labored daily in prayer for me throughout the process and who continue to do so. My pastors have not only been my loving sister and brother in Christ, but they have been like parents to me, showing unconditional love, support, and concern for my professional and spiritual growth and development. I am grateful to them for being pastors after the heart of God who feeds his people with knowledge and understanding (Jeremiah 3:15).

I am grateful to my former mentors, Drs. Charles von Urff and Thomas Chamberlain, and to my current mentor, Dr. Diane Gavin, and my dissertation committee members, Drs. Brenda Curry and Ann Deaton, who very generously contributed their valuable time, expertise, and knowledge to ensure my work was one of quality and worthiness. I thank them for their diligence and dedication to my work and my success.

My thanks must also go to the many friends, colleagues, and co-workers who supported me along the way in many different ways. I thank my good friend, former teaching partner, and Senior Naval Science Instructor Douglas Cook, LCDR, USN (ret.), and his wife Leah for their undying friendship and support. Many thanks also to all of the Navy Junior Reserve Officer Training Corps (NJROTC) cadets whom I have had the privilege of knowing, teaching, and training and who were a tremendous part of the inspiration for this work. I thank Lucinda Probst from Bremerton High school in Bremerton, Washington, for her invaluable support in the way of transcription services for my dissertation, and math teacher Mr. Steve Crumb who advised and tutored me in statistics during the third year of the doctoral program. I also thank my current co-workers and fellow Naval Science Instructors at

Central High School in Brooksville, Florida, Michael Ralph, Lt Col, USMC (Ret.), and Bruce Kennedy, MC, USN (Ret.), for their encouragement, support, and understanding as I labored through the final phases of the program into the home stretch.

TABLE OF CONTENTS

LIST OF TABLES

LIST OF FIGURES

CHAPTER 1: INTRODUCTION

The terrorist attacks on America on September 11, 2001, brought global recognition to a group of people who embrace a devastating philosophy previously unheard of in modern society (Chamberlain 2007); a political philosophy demanding the conformation of governments to its own perception of Islamic law. These events demonstrated to the American public and to the world at large the reality and the magnitude of the al-Qa'ida threat not only against the United States but also against global targets (Parrish 2006). The events of that day in September 2001 significantly altered the American people's perspective concerning all aspects of a strategy for homeland defense (Burns 2003).

The national quest for military men and women guided by exceptional core values and ethics who are heroic in their efforts prompted the present research study. The goal of the present study was to explore such values and ethics and to consider whether or not the "sword and shield" approaches (Toner 2006, 1) could be integrated effectively amidst the unconventional dynamics of the 21st century Global War on Terrorism (GWOT). Chapter 1 includes a thorough discussion of the background circumstances that warrant an investigation of the problem under research. The specific problem, the need for the study, and the selected study population are identified. The chapter also includes the purpose, significance, and nature of the study. Chapter 1 also introduces the research questions that were used to guide the investigation and the theoretical framework providing the perspective from which the problem was approached. Operational terms and those used in unconventional manners in the study have been defined, and assumptions, scope, limitations, and delimitations of the study are discussed.

Background of the Problem

Operation Iraqi Freedom was launched March 20, 2003, as America, supported by allies, responded with decisive military might in pursuing the Global War on Terrorism (GWOT) (Helm 2006; Holdstock 2001). In doing so, America's leadership role and stance in the global conflict precipitated unfavorable perceptions of the U.S. Armed Forces, both domestically and internationally (Gerges 2004). With the onset of the GWOT, the need for exceptional military leadership blending ethical and military competencies and enhanced training forums has become crucial for national security (Francis 2008; Toner 2006).

In the exercise of 21st century counterterrorist measures following September 11, 2001, three requirements were crucial, each centering on the quality of leadership (Avishag 2006; Kondrasuk, Bailey, & Sheeks 2005; Toner 2006). First was the requirement for leaders who were not only fearless and focused on battlefield victory, but who were also committed to the preservation of military ethical conventions. Avishag termed these conventions "purity of arms" (493), which call for moral behavior in warfare. Equally important was the requirement for informed leaders clearly aware of the background and history of global terrorism and the need for an effective response to its devastating effects (Kondrasuk et al. 2005). The third, and most important requirement, was for trained leaders committed to improving and enhancing the nobility, integrity, and dignity of human service (Toner 2006), even amidst the contemporary climate of terrorism. The present study was designed to address questions about the values, virtues, leadership style, and morals that, when combined, produce 21st century warriors with the capacity to defend vigorously while adhering relentlessly to a high moral code.

In many ways, strangely similar to the historic date of December 7, 1941, September 11, 2001, (dubbed 9/11) became another "day that will live in infamy" (Franklin Delano Roosevelt, 1941 as cited in U.S. Historical Documents, 2008). The mantra "Remember Pearl Harbor," in 1941 became "Remember 9/11," in 2001. Terrorist attacks on the New York World Trade Center that day had sparked the GWOT. The mantra, "Remember 9/11," faded rapidly amidst the fear and anxiety of the prospect of war— a war some Americans soon labeled an "immoral and illegal war" (Jensen 2003). Americans had become more keenly aware of military affairs, the way the military conducted its business, and the image of the American military at home and abroad (Huddy, Feldman, Taber, & Lahav 2005).

Aside from the questions that were raised concerning a balance between security and liberty (Simon 2003; Weinberg, Eubank, & Francis 2008), a major consequence of 9/11 was that the GWOT fostered demands that the military also focus intense efforts on the priority of nation building. Such efforts were intended to help dispel the anxieties aroused by public scrutiny, both at home and abroad (Gerges 2004). The military must not only train leaders to adapt and adjust to a "fundamentally changed security environment," but at the same time, lead frontline troops into battle in an unconventional war (Donahoe 2004, 1).

The changing face of the battlefield resulting from the GWOT presented situations not previously encountered by the U.S. military in armed conflict. These situations have subsequently changed some of the ways in which American forces conduct warfare and have even prompted recent rewriting and editing of the Army and Marine Corps counterinsurgency manual (Peters 2007). Such situations require transformation-oriented leaders who will prepare the U.S. military to be a situation-relevant and ready force, capable of meeting the demands of a new kind of battlefield, a unique foe, and a highly involved and opinionated social and political arena (Secretary of the Army 2006). In this arena, the frontline service members, who present the first impression of America abroad, face harsh scrutiny due to dissipating political domestic and international support for deployed American forces (Gerges 2004). In spite of the legitimacy of such scrutiny, the reality of the substantially asymmetrical nature of contemporary armed conflict raises unique issues addressed by international law and demanding close examination (Helm 2006).

The reality of 21st century warfare has outpaced the traditional requirements of the Law of Armed Conflict (LOAC) (Bailey 2006; Helm 2006). The emerging complexities have presented significant challenges prompting military planners to reexamine former practices for use in unique contemporary battlefield situations (Minaudo 2009). Such battlefield conditions further justify and warrant the need for research into effective contemporary military leadership styles and philosophy.

Since the events of September 11, 2001, the image of America has undergone extremely harsh scrutiny, criticism, and ridicule, both domestically and internationally (Gerges 2004). Gerges indicated many Americans have expressed concern about the nation's threatened loss of world leadership and reputation abroad, placing this as the main priority and motivation for change in military practices, policies, and the way in which the business of the nation is carried out. Some people fear that America's involvements in foreign affairs, such as the war in Iraq, have reaped dangerous and unanticipated consequences (Theros 2003). Still others are preoccupied with the debate over the need for U.S. border security and pursuant issues. During this period, President George W. Bush issued warnings against following the broad and inviting road of isolationism and protectionism in a complex and challenging time (2006).

Such domestic differences, coupled with major international protests a year into the conflict, fostered a political divide over the role the government and ultimately the military should play in world conflicts (Twair & Powell 2004). For instance, according to Torr (2005, 1), President George W. Bush released a statement declaring the United States should join allies to encourage "international nonproliferation and arms reduction," especially weapons of mass destruction, with which some on both sides of the political divide might agree. Torr suggested the controversy arises with the President's suggestion that the United States may find it necessary to employ preemptive military strikes in its effort to eliminate such threats. Opinions have been voiced supporting preemption only in the event of an imminent attack and decrying its use to any degree in the GWOT (Sterngold 2004).

Some people argue that preemptive armed force in certain situations such as peace operations (PO), which include peace keeping operations (PKO) and peace enforcement operations (PEO), is not necessarily to be held in reserve for use as a last resort despite efforts and desire to preserve *just war theory* (Wester 2007). These and many other questions, considerations, opinions, and differences increase the political divide, leaving the military awkwardly straddled between the two sides and exposed to criticism. In the wake of that criticism, military leaders face the challenge of providing not just strategic and operational leadership but also moral and ethical leadership (Hartle 2007). They must adhere to and preserve a high code of military virtues and conduct originating with military customs, courtesies, and traditions developed throughout the history of armed forces and armed conflict (Dion 2007). They must simultaneously maintain civility, loyalty, and allegiance to the country and must pass on those values in real and compelling ways to those over whom they have charge.

Even good military leaders' motives, morals, ethics, and actions are sometimes questioned (Torr 2005). The questioning, and often dissent, while epitomizing the very nature of a free and just society (Kalb 2003) can be unjustly motivated by the objective of fault-finding. Military leaders must consequently adhere to a strong code of ethics and responsibility, remaining beyond reproach and mindful that the resources they expend and protect are human lives (*Leading Marines FMFM1-0*, n.d. as cited by Shriberg, Shriberg, & Lloyd 2002).

Ethics refers to anything that pertains to the correct behavior of individuals and their attitude toward others, their God, and themselves (*Encyclopedia of Spiritual Knowledge*, n.d.). Ethical leadership behavior occurs when a leader takes an action specifically in observance of a distinct standard of conduct (MCWP 6-11, 2002) and overcomes a conflicting moral dilemma. Morals pertain to the concepts of good and bad, and how a person behaves accordingly and consequently (*Encyclopedia of Spiritual Knowledge*, n.d.). Over time, morals evolve into societal traditions (mores) to which the entire group unquestioningly ascribes (Advameg 2009). Moral principles are subjective; ethics are objective (*Encyclopedia of Spiritual Knowledge*, n.d.). Values are deeply held beliefs usually accumulated from childhood and unchanged over time (Looper 2007). According to Looper (2007), values are personal; they do not concern what is right or wrong, but rather what is right for the individual.

Religious education often establishes a foundation for good morals, ethics, and values (Brunei Times 2009). Reference group theory, a component of social learning theory, supports the contention that religion deters crime (Hercik et al. 2005). The extant body of research indicated that rising crime statistics are due to a lack of religious beliefs/moral values abounding in contemporary society (Hercik et al. 2005). Logic points to the reasoning behind this as failure to integrate religious concepts into training in both family and institutional educations. The military, as any other segment of American society, has its share of leaders who create a "moral standards gap" (Rice 2005, n.p.) which impacts the quality of the fighting force.

Winning hearts and minds has often been identified as the justification for American military actions abroad. The primary objective has been to reduce anti-American sentiment (the fuel of terrorism), thereby making America and the world safer for its citizens (Greenwald 2006). The objective of winning hearts and minds cannot be adequately accomplished without a sophisticated and demonstrated understanding of the situation (Supervielle 2005) and the culture of the country to include its religious mores and foundations. American troops receive limited formal education concerning the impact of the Islamic religion on the law of war (Supervielle 2005). Because of this lack of understanding, troops and commanders may encounter situations in which their actions (and often their words) run counter to their objectives with serious ramifications. Recommendations for military training in how to function optimally in operational environments where religion is a critical element in the makeup of the society have surfaced amid the dynamics of the GWOT (Carlson 2008).

Such outlined challenges present both the contemporary and the historical framework within which American military leaders are compelled and obligated to lead and to train young troops and future leaders.

The difficulties military leaders confront are compounded when young impressionable troops must make value judgments and withstand political and social attacks on their personal character and convictions (Swiatek 2005). This type of challenge demands leaders instill in followers not only military skill and prowess but also enduring values and unswerving moral judgment to confront the ethical situations and dilemmas they face daily (Verweij, Hofhuis, & Soeters 2007).

Statement of the Problem

World affairs in the 21st century and increased diversity in the nature of military missions have placed responsibilities on the U.S. military, demanding a strict military ethos and code and unparalleled leadership ethics, principles, methods, and practices (Matthew, Cianciola, & Sternberg 2005; Toner 2006). According to Toner (2006), moral failure of the troops is deeply rooted in the failure of leaders. High standards of personal conduct and moral character are key concepts in successful leadership, and exemplify the most important military leadership principle–leading by example (Bantu-Gomez 2004; Sluiberg et al. 2002).

The specific problem addressed in the present study was the need for credible qualified leaders for a 21st century military (Defense and the National Interest 2007). The goal of the study, using a qualitative grounded theory approach, was to determine and share the values that account for the success of exceptional military leaders. Without the advantages of such a body of information, military leaders have no visible proven examples to follow and apply to personal practice (Wren 2005). The general population included senior enlisted members of the U.S. military.

Purpose of the Study

The purpose of the present qualitative grounded theory research was to create a model based on the exploration of the values that guide and influence the style and practices of successful military leaders. The study was structured to use currently collected data derived from eight proven successful military leaders who were the primary participants in the study. Secondary participants were individuals, *not being studied,* who were acquainted with the military leaders, including mentors, followers, and peers, who had knowledge of the leaders. Historical data were also collected and analyzed. The results of the study were used to develop a theory that explains the success of military leaders with respect to the values they hold. The emerging data were also used to create and describe a model to be used by leaders in addressing the goal of developing a force committed to ethical perspectives and values. These ethics, when more clearly defined, undergird, strengthen, and support the leadership of the American military.

Senior enlisted U.S. military members comprised the general population in the present study. Eight leaders (seven men and one woman) who hold or who previously held billets as the senior enlisted member of a military command or military service comprised the specific primary sample group. The goal of the research study was to create a theoretical model grounded in the data and emerging from an exploration of the specific values that influence and guide the style and practices of successful military leaders.

Significance of the Study

According to Bruno and Lay (2006), personal value systems, once internalized, whether consciously or unconsciously, form the foundation and establish the criteria that guide one's actions. The values concept may be the most crucial underlying determinant of leaders' behavior and is an important factor in the study of leadership. Researchers have produced ample literature and studies on the subject of leadership and military leadership, but only a limited number have been focused on isolating the specific values that contribute to military leadership success in the 21st century. Considering the moral and ethical challenges inherent in the life of 21st century military personnel, values become even more critical for leaders. Benefiting both researchers in the field of leadership as well as leadership practitioners, the present study represents a unique approach to the problem addressed in the study.

Significance of the Study to the Field of Leadership

Research indicated that, to date, no widely accepted comprehensive theory concerning effective leadership exists (Johnson & Hill 2009). The literature review for the present study revealed an insignificant amount of existing literature regarding the specific personal and professional values that influence and contribute to the success of military leadership. The lack of academic attention to this topic has resulted in a misuse and mismanagement of military leadership training efforts and resources because both have focused on unproven methods that do not address values-based leadership training for leaders and followers (Johnson & Hill 2009).

The significance and unique contribution of the present study to the field of leadership and the body of leadership literature is twofold. The study was designed to focus on and identify specific values that contribute to successful military leadership as revealed in the data. The study culminated in the development and creation of a values-based model. The model aligns theory and practice by depicting a holistic and humanistic leadership foundation from which values associated with leadership emerge, and the alignment of those values with actions, practices and behaviors of the leaders.

An additional contribution the research effort makes to current and future studies and thought lies in its potential to provide to military leaders visible and documented examples of how to lead effectively in a challenging postmodern military force of 21st century warfare. The information may be of valuable and practical use in influencing and guiding actions and shaping values of young recruits who, after accession, go on to become military leaders themselves (Swiatek 2005). The study results are applicable to all organizations and personal leadership scenarios because leadership is about people and events and is transferable and adaptable to various situations (Prewitt 2004; Yeakey 2002).

Nature of the Study

Qualitative research relies upon observation and the participants' views, as opposed to a researcher's personal opinions or paradigm (Berg &

Latin 2007; Creswell 2005). For the present study, letters inviting top-level enlisted military leaders were sent to individuals inviting them to participate in the study. The letter was accompanied by the informed consent form. Those military leaders willing to participate were asked to contact the researcher to arrange a mutually convenient time for an interview. The interview protocol involved a semi-structured interview lasting approximately an hour. The military leaders were asked to name someone who would serve as a secondary participant to comment upon their leadership style and activities. The secondary participants were then contacted, asked to complete the informed consent form, and scheduled for an interview at a mutually convenient time.

Broad questions were asked and data consisting mainly of text were gathered through an interview process in the present qualitative grounded theory study. The content was then described and analyzed in an unbiased manner for emerging themes that led to answers to the research questions. In accordance with the Creswell (2005) description of qualitative research, inquiry was conducted in a subjective manner. From the views of the participants, a detailed understanding of the participants' leadership values, actions, practices and behaviors, and leadership style preferences were derived. Broad general questions were posed, providing complete openness, as suggested by Creswell. The data were collected primarily in the form of text, and were described and analyzed for any themes that were evident.

Overview of Research Method Appropriateness

Quantitative studies emphasize "the measurement and analysis of causal relationships between variables," whereas qualitative studies emphasize the quality of entities and processes and meanings not experimentally examined (Denzin & Lincoln 2005, 10). A qualitative method was chosen rather than a quantitative method because the present study was designed to explore the themes and patterns relative to the primary participants' leadership behavior and principles. A quantitative method would have been used to measure the relationships between known variables. The variables (which were unknown) were the focus of the inquiry, which justified qualitative research as the appropriate method. The relatively small sample resulted from purposive (judgmental) rather than random (probability) sampling. The purposive sample was chosen because of the need for participants who would be appropriate for the study. The available population of military leaders with the level of expertise and success required for the purpose of the study was limited.

A qualitative method was the preferred method for gaining a closer perspective on the individual's point of view through in-depth interviews and observation (Denzin & Lincoln 2005). Berg and Latin (2007) asserted that a qualitative study is an open-ended, flexible approach to inquiry that asks interview questions focusing on what, how, and other contextual details of the phenomena studied. The present qualitative study was structured to ask questions pertaining to the personal and professional values held by the participants; the specific actions, practices, and behaviors that proved successful for the participants; and how both common and unique leadership challenges were confronted and overcome. The study goals were accomplished by way of extensive, intense interviews with the participants and with those influenced by personal experiences with them (Seidman 2006). The results of the interviews were used to develop a theory concerning the specific values that influence and guide the practices of successful military leaders.

Qualitative research is a method of research that facilitates the ability to describe activities and results rather than quantitatively and numerically measuring outcomes and results (Creswell 2005; Guion & Flowers 2008). The objective is to facilitate lucid sharing of the information deemed valuable and useful. During the conduct of qualitative research, according to Creswell, the problems must be explored to gain deeper insight into the concept or issue. In the present qualitative study, an exploration of the research problem through the eyes, the thoughts, and the reasoning of the participants provided deeper understanding of the problem and presented leadership solutions.

Glaser and Strauss (1967) noted that with the use of qualitative measures, a sense of ownership in the project results when the research participants become knowledgeably and actively involved in the process as the primary source of information and data. A sense of participant ownership increased the validity and the importance of the research, thus enhancing the ability to accomplish the study goals. A sense of ownership also generated participant support for the initiative and the goals of the research, leading to the most effective conclusions and solutions (Rabinowitz & Berkowitz 2009).

Effective leadership style, some theorists argue, depends ultimately on the observer, the situation, and the people involved (Ruderman 2008). The goal of the study was to investigate the values, leadership style, and practices of senior enlisted military leaders in personal and professional interactional leadership situations. The results of the study were to be used to build a theory that describes and explains the values that account for the success of military leadership. The focus of the study and the resultant theory was on revealing and determining how and why the leaders' values and belief systems influenced their practices as proven and successful leaders (Cooper & Schindler 2006). To strengthen the emergent theory, the data were supported and corroborated by the views and perspectives of other pertinent study participants (Murray 2008).

Such objectives required a study design that allowed the participants to tell the story, providing "rich descriptive detail" (Trochim 2006, 3) that ultimately led to the answers sought. A qualitative research design was appropriate and best suited to this objective because it facilitated the ability to place more emphasis on greater contextual analysis of limited conditions and events (Creswell 2005). The examination and investigation of the details of the phenomenon were able to be studied more intensely and with greater focus.

Overview of Research Design Appropriateness

A qualitative approach aided in the discovery not only of the values contributing to leadership success, but also how and why they are effective (Cooper & Schindler 2006). Four major types of qualitative research design include (a) phenomenology, (b) ethnology, (c) case study, and (d) grounded theory (Bitsch 2005; Hancock 2002) Grounded theory was the selected research design for the study. Grounded theory is considered an "emergent methodology" (Dick 2005, 2), implying that the theory developed from the research is grounded in the data from which it was derived (Dick 2005; Glaser & Strauss 1967). Military leaders comprised the general population in the present study. A qualitative grounded theory approach to the study of the leadership experiences of successful military leaders was intended to reveal a detailed description of the values that guide and influence the style and practices of such leaders.

The grounded theory research design relies upon raw data collected from the participants to develop a theory emerging from the meaning of the data, to provide an understanding of a situation (Dick 2005). The data were not subject to any previous theoretical conceptions and constructions of what was expected (Creswell 2005; Murray 2008). Dick suggested constant data comparison was an essential element for the success of the methodology and the research process. A grounded theory research design was appropriate for the study because it allowed a theory concerning successful leadership values to emerge from the information derived from the data collected from the leaders. The study resulted in a model that explains how and why exemplary leadership style and preferences are developed and what values influence them (Cooper & Schindler 2006).

Several qualitative research design approaches can be used to explore leadership characteristics and values (Barbuto 2005; Kamil 2004). One goal of the present study was to generate a theory that emerged from or that was grounded in the data collected (Glaser & Strauss 1967) that pertained to the personal and professional values of the participants. The stated goals of grounded theory research contrast with the goals of case studies, which merely describe what the subjects do; ethnographic studies describe the people or the culture being investigated; and phenomenological studies describe something that exists in the world such as events, experiences, or concepts (Trent Focus Group 2002).

Theory in quantitative research is logical and typically deductive, whereas qualitative theory tends to be largely inductive, investigating themes and classifying and cataloging data (Saddler 2007). Grounded theory, according to Burns and Grove (2005) is an inductive technique in research that facilitates building theory around and pertaining to a specific topic of interest. The goal of the present study included the creation of a practical, theoretical model for the alignment of theory and practice that identifies and describes the values that influence and guide successful military leaders. Consumers consequently benefit from a theory produced inductively and grounded in the data-driven information derived from knowledgeable informants.

Research Questions

Qualitative research begins with a broad or central question and gathers data from several sources to include archival records, documents, observations, interviews, and physical artifacts (Cohen & Crabtree 2008; Creswell 2005, 2007; Dick 2005; Hancock 2002). Sub-questions guide the research to specific answers that satisfy the broad, overarching question. Central research questions may be divided into four categories: descriptive, exploratory, explanatory, and emancipatory (Marshall & Rossman 2006).

The central research question for the present study was designed to follow the line of questioning consistent with the descriptive and explanatory categories. The goal and the primary focus of the study were to reveal, describe, and explain the values causal to successful leadership practices. The assertion that a positive relationship exists between personal and professional values and leadership effectiveness and success (Bruno & Lay 2006) undergird the theoretical foundation of the study. The focus of the research questions was not on exploring if a relationship existed, but rather on revealing the nature of the values contributing to leadership success.

Research Question 1

The broad overarching research question used to direct the study concerned the guiding values and influences of the leaders studied. Successful leaders create a culture driven by certain intrinsic values that become platforms for calls to action and not merely empty platitudes (DiMatteo 2007). Such a leader earns the right to leadership through legitimacy of power enhanced by concern for the well-being, welfare, training, and readiness of troops as opposed to self-serving goals and aspirations. The goal was that the results of the research would reveal the source and type of the values that inform and guide the practices of such leaders. Two more specific questions explored and described specific situations and circumstances in which the leaders achieved success in accomplishing leadership objectives by adhering to a proclaimed value system. A fourth research question pertained to likely theoretical leadership models that might be applied effectively to military leadership based on the claims of the leaders.

RQ1: What specific personal and professional values inform and sway the opinions and practices of successful military leaders in accomplishing the highly essential and important duties and the responsibilities of the leadership roles they hold as senior enlisted advisors to organizational commanders?

Research Question 2

The second question concerned specific actions and practices of the leaders. Le Pla and Roberts (2004) suggested that the secret to successful leadership may lie not in who a leader is or what the leader claims to be, but in what the leader does. For this reason, specific and citable actions that supported and substantiated any claims made were sought and investigated. Research Question 2 explored congruency between espoused theory and theory in practice: praxis (Smith, M. 2000). The objective of this discovery process was to present evidence by way of personal actions accounting for the success of the leaders.

RQ2: What specific actions, practices, and behaviors account for the success and recognition the leaders experience in capturing the loyalty, honor, and respect from superiors, followers, and peers alike?

Research Question 3

Organizational leaders face challenges in many forms. The challenges of the information technology industry during its formative years have been daunting (Hoving 2007), but those challenges pale in comparison to those presented by human interactional issues within organizations.

The third research question was used to discover how leaders dealt with those challenges, both anticipated and unexpected. Kouzes and Posner (2007) described five challenges that good leaders must face and be prepared to address using certain identified methods, and they listed behavioral commitments leaders must make to meet those challenges. To identify the leadership practices of the participants, the five exemplary leader practices as identified by Kouzes and Posner was considered. The practices are "model the way, inspire a shared vision, challenge the process, enable others to act, and encourage the heart" (Kouzes & Posner 2007, 3.)

RQ3: How did the leaders meet the challenges of leadership that all leaders face, from dealing with followers who oppose and resist leadership actions and processes to building up those who need encouragement?

Research Question 4

The autocratic style of leadership and management typically associated with military leaders and managers is gradually being replaced by less formal styles based on persuasion and influence rather than organizational position and status (McCrimmon 2007). McCrimmon stated that this may be due in part to a modern trend toward "thought leadership" and leadership by example (n.p). With this in mind, the study explored the specific existing leadership theories and models evident in the styles of the participants as effective and successful military leaders.

RQ4: What existing theoretical leadership models account for and explain the organizational performance of successful military leaders?

The data collected in the present research study provided insights into the values that guide and influence successful leaders in meeting the social, training, and developmental needs of troops, both in garrison and in conventional and unconventional combat battlefield situations. The implications of the study were applied to the development of a generic leadership model meeting the stated objective.

Theoretical Framework

The purpose of the present qualitative grounded theory research was to create a model based on the exploration of the values that guide and influence the style and practices of successful military leaders. Military leadership is the subject of much discussion and literature of late due to the prevailing national defense and homeland security climate in the United States (Defense Technical Information Center 2007; Randall 2006). Several competing and harmonizing concepts and theories impact the concept of military leadership. The unique influence of the GWOT on contemporary military leadership renders many such concepts and theories insufficient to explain leadership success in this context.

Beyond the specific context and impact of the GWOT on military leadership, the unique requirements of military operations in themselves suggest considerations not treated in existing models, thus the models often are insufficient to explain military success. For instance, battlefield situations require leaders to react and make decisions not only instantaneously but also with much confidence and conviction, considering the grave responsibilities for the life and safety of other people. Excluding civilian safety and peace-keeping forces, rarely is such the case in non-military organizations. Although the study was designed to focus on the theoretical area of military leadership within the specific context of the GWOT, other relevant and supporting topics and issues were included to establish a more complete framework. A brief look at some ethical, moral, and value theories also helps complete the framework.

Factors Influencing 21st Century Military Leadership

Government agencies and scholars have generated a wide array of studies describing individual factors assumed to influence the global terrorist threat against the United States and its allies since the terrorist attacks of September 11, 2001 (Fatur 2005). Within the studies are numerous issues, perspectives, and controversies that merit consideration and discussion, including medical issues such as managing post-traumatic stress disorder in veterans returning from the GWOT (Lambert

2006). In the social sciences discipline, Cavaleri (2005) explored theories surrounding the applicability and the evolution of the corpus constituting the law of war. Other more pertinent issues included leadership and military retention rate, leadership styles, female leadership in the military, leadership ethics, leadership reporting issues, and the impact of the GWOT upon the morale and reputation of American troops.

Retention rate. The results of a study of clinical laboratory scientists conducted by Bamberg, Akroyd, and Moore (2008) supported the position that leadership behaviors were definite predictors of personnel retention. In the military arena, Abrashoff (2001) and Randall (2006) surmised that leadership success through the development of key leadership skills can be a major indicator of military retention rate. Many studies cite military retention rate as a sign of effective leadership and quality leaders (Abrashoff 2001). According to Abrashoff, 40% of the new recruits entering the navy's basic training program will not complete their initial 4-year tour of duty.

If the above statistic is any indication of the retention rate across all the armed services, one could only speculate that the quality of leadership available to today's armed forces is a major factor contributing to this situation. Academic research indicated that much of the crisis in retention is related to the behavior of leaders (Kleinman 2004; Lock 2003; Randall 2006). Maintaining quality leadership should be a major focus of the military forces over the coming years. A concerted effort to place important emphasis on leadership and leadership skills training and development is expected to result in a decrease in attrition rates (Defense and the National Interest 2007, n.p.).

The severity and urgency of the crisis regarding the need for effective, able, and adaptable military leadership is evident, especially in the post-9/11 environment and the ensuing Global War on Terror (Mueller-Hansen, White, Dorsey, & Pulakos 2005). Whether the crisis is unusual or commonplace, and whatever the solutions, one thing is certain: bad leadership has a detrimental effect on military retention rates (Abrashoff 2001; Randall 2006), which affects the readiness and effectiveness of the military forces. The application of effective leadership models resulting from research such as the present study can address and potentially reverse this crisis.

Leadership styles. Some studies on leadership, especially military leadership, highlight specific leadership characteristics, features, and situations (Thomsong 2004). Some military leadership studies express the need to discover new ways of training, in new places, on new tasks, to meet the requirements of a new and rapidly changing combat environment (Darken & Sadagic 2006). In the present study, the influence of effective leadership values and styles on personal and unit performance, as discussed by Willenz (2003), was briefly considered.

Female leadership in the military. A controversial leadership topic with differing perspectives, addressed by Wilson (2005) and Putko and Johnson (2008), is that of the female leader in the military. Although the place of the female military leader in the past has been a somewhat contentious subject, recent years have seen the issue receive less scrutiny and debate as women prove themselves highly capable and adaptable to a military lifestyle, as noted by Wilson and Putko and Johnson. The perception of the female military leader by her peers, leaders, and followers often affect the leader's responses to leadership challenges and decisions. In spite of the advances in female combat and leadership participation in the armed services, the realization that women still face many challenges in the struggle for recognition and higher leadership status has been often noted (Ackmann 2003; Looney, Kurpius, & Lucart 2004). Regardless of the recent upturn in women attaining higher leadership and managerial positions, some indications are that women are still (at the time of this writing) disproportionately absent in the upper echelon of both the military and business worlds (Jandeska & Kraimer 2005; Looney, 2004; Looney et al. 2004; Sumner & Niederman 2004).

Leadership ethics. Military leadership ethics is another issue within the theoretical and conceptual framework of this study. According to Pfaff (2002), all military leaders inevitably make ethics decisions. Although this observation may not be controversial, Pfaff suggested selecting the best method to resolve the challenges brought about by ethical problems can be a daunting challenge for military leaders. Technological advancement, enhanced communications capabilities, and rapidly changing battle and strategic conditions create an operational environment that calls for rapid decision making and sustained momentum once it has been achieved (Jaszlics, Sanders, & Culkin 2006). Such capacity must be tempered with sound logic and ethical decision making to resolve conflicts in a consistent and rational manner.

Leadership reporting issues. According to Dodd (2004), one of the problems confronting military leadership is the less-than-accurate reporting of leaders' actions by both the press and media consumers. A large portion of the problem stems from the fact that many American media consumers engage in exchanges about military leadership without clearly understanding the nature of military leadership. What is worse, according to Dodd, is that many of those who write about military leadership do so from uninformed positions of ignorance. Because most Americans rely on media sources for military operations information, the quality of reporting on military leadership has become an important issue to the military, especially because the American public is capable of monitoring worldwide operations against U.S. adversaries such as al Qa'ida in the GWOT.

GWOT impact upon troop morale and welfare. Lack of integrity and morality within the military can be a serious strategic leadership issue (Muskoff 2006) with unfortunate and unintended consequences. Intense public observation and scrutiny of the performance of the American military in the GWOT has revealed numerous alleged and actual immoral and unscrupulous acts of indiscretion that might have been avoided or mitigated with proper attention to the leadership and training of troops (Rivkin 2004). The unique nature of the GWOT, coupled with 21st century media coverage, spotlights such acts in a way that has not heretofore been possible (McLane 2004). Although the possibility exists that such indiscretions also occurred in former military conflicts, the means to publicize them instantaneously were absent.

New and advanced media and public communications technology has made instant publication of military activities and heightened enemy capabilities in contemporary conflicts possible (Caldwell, Murphy, & Menning 2009). Such technology includes the popular *YouTube*, *Myspace*, *Facebook*, and *Twitter* social networking Web sites with video-sharing capability, Web cameras, instant text and voice messaging devices, cell phones, friendly and adversarial satellite networks, and American military media imbeds (Caldwell et al. 2009; McLane 2004). Rivkin (2004) observed that the advent of new technology ushers the frontlines of the war directly into homes around the world, widening the sphere of military exposure and further justifying the demand for quality training. For this reason, the quality and extent of American military victory depends heavily upon not just whether or not wars are won, but how they are won (Capizzi & Holmes 2008). The manner in which wars are fought and won affects the ability of troops to withstand criticism and negative exposure in the way of daily attacks upon their values, virtues, morals, and personal convictions (Swiatek 2005).

Behavioral Approaches to Ethical Decision Making
Ethics has been a philosophical focus for thousands of years. The resulting moral philosophies (or ethical theories) form the foundation for contemporary business ethics (Advameg 2009, n.p.). According to Advameg, Inc. (2009), some of the foremost theories are related to business ethics and ethical decision making. They include teleology, which focuses on the consequences of actions (e.g. egoism and utilitarianism); deontology, which focuses on individual rights and the actor's intent; justice, which focuses on fairness to the affected individual/s; and relativism, which focuses on subjective judgment and may vary from one person, group, or culture to the next.

Military leaders, especially in contemporary warfare such as the GWOT, inevitably face ethical dilemmas on a daily basis (Pfaff 2002). Balancing the demands of moral and professional concerns require that they make decisions that best enhance their effectiveness as leaders. A solid understanding of ethical behavioral theories supports values-based leadership styles and practices.

Definition of Terms

The meanings of terminology used in the present document in a non-standard manner are clarified in this section. Also included are definitions clarifying important terms relative to the study that provide a means of limitation and focus for the study. The clarifying definitions include citations of standard, commonly used meanings for the terms ethics, values, and morals.

Bearing: In this study, *bearing* is conducting oneself in a professional manner, displaying alertness, competence, confidence, and personal control. Bearing also signifies fitness and proper military appearance (Department of the Army 2006; "Marine Corps Leadership Traits" 2007). A leader's bearing has significant influence on subordinates (Air Force Doctrine Document 1-1 2006). The *ArmyStudyGuide* (2008) described military bearing in terms of command presence and presenting a professional reflection of authority.

Commandant of the Marine Corps (CMC): Unique to the United States Marine Corps, this title refers to the Marine member of the JCS. The CMC is the highest-ranking member of the United States Marine Corps, is appointed by the President, and reports to the Secretary of the Navy (SECNAV) (Answers Corporation 2009).

Courage: Courage refers to the quality that allows one to face fear in a calm, rational manner. Physical courage means being able to function effectively in the presence of physical danger. Mental courage refers to the mental and moral strength to support what is right (Department of the Army 2006; "Marine Corps Leadership Traits" 2007). A person of high moral courage will do the right thing without regard to personal cost (Air Force Doctrine Document 1-1 2006).

Decisiveness: Decisiveness refers to the "ability to make good decisions without delay. Get all the facts and weigh them against each other. By acting calmly and quickly, you should arrive at a sound decision. You announce your decisions in a clear, firm, professional manner" ("Marine Corps Leadership Traits" 2007, n.p.). Decisiveness is a tool used by leaders to influence subordinates (Air Force Doctrine Document 1-1 2006).

Dependability: Dependability means reliability in the proper performance of duties—that one can be trusted to complete a job. Dependability is the willing and voluntary support of the policies and orders of the chain of command. Dependability also means consistently putting forth one's best effort in an attempt to achieve the highest standards of performance ("Marine Corps Leadership Traits" 2007, n.p.).

Endurance: Endurance refers to "the mental and physical stamina that is measured by the ability to withstand pain, fatigue, stress, and hardship. For example, enduring pain during a conditioning march in order to improve stamina is crucial in the development of leadership" ("Marine Corps Leadership Traits" 2007, n.p.).

Enthusiasm: Enthusiasm is described as "a sincere interest and exuberance in the performance of duties; Optimistic, cheerful, and willing to accept the challenges" ("Marine Corps Leadership Traits" 2007, n.p.).

Ethics: Ethics refers to well-founded standards of right and wrong, prescribing what people ought to do, normally in terms of rights, obligations, societal benefits, justness, or explicit virtues (Velasquez, Andre, Shanks & Meyer 2008). According to Velasquez et al. (2008), ethics also refers to the study, practice, and development of one's own ethical standards.

Initiative: Initiative is the ability to act in the absence of orders. Initiative also means speaking up to contribute technical knowledge and information and resourcefulness in the accomplishment of goals when normal materials and means are unavailable (Department of the Army 2006; "Marine Corps Leadership Traits" 2007).

Inspiration: The term refers to the military quality of exhibiting a "personal example of high moral standards reflecting virtue, honor, patriotism, and subordination in personal behavior and in performance" ("Leadership" 1980, n.p.).

Integrity: Integrity means displaying honesty and acting legally and morally at all times, even when no one is watching. People of integrity put honesty, duty, and sound moral principles first (Air Force Doctrine Document 1-1 2006; Department of the Army 2006; "Marine Corps Leadership Traits" 2007).

Judgment: Judgment refers to the ability to assess situations calmly and shrewdly to make good decisions (Department of the Army 2006; "Marine Corps Leadership Traits" 2007).

Justice: "Marine Corps Leadership Traits" (2007, n.p.) described justice as "practice of being fair and consistent. A just person gives consideration to each side of a situation and bases rewards or punishments on merit." Air Force Doctrine Document 1-1 (2006) describes justice as treating people fairly and acting with a fundamental awareness of the worth of all people.

Knowledge: Knowledge is "the understanding of a science or art. Knowledge means that one has acquired information and that one understands people" ("Marine Corps Leadership Traits" 2007). Knowledge includes domain knowledge, tactical knowledge, technical knowledge, and cultural/geopolitical knowledge (Department of the Army 2006).

Loyalty: Loyalty refers to devotion to the country, military service, and the Constitution. Loyalty also refers to faithfulness to subordinates, peers, and leaders, both up and down the chain of command (Air Force Doctrine Document 1-1 2006; Department of the Army 2006; "Marine Corps Leadership Traits" 2007).

Military leaders: Military leaders include mainly, although not exclusively, Staff Noncommissioned Officers (SNCOs). These enlisted men and women are often referred to as the backbone of any military service (Estes 2008) and are chiefly responsible not only for the basic training of enlisted personnel, but also for the initial training of officer candidates while they attend Officer Candidate School (OCS).

Moral responsibility: Moral responsibility refers to the military discipline of "personal adherence to high standards of conduct and the guidance of subordinates toward wholesomeness of mind and body" ("Leadership" 1980, n.p.).

Morals: Morals involve the human behavior that a society or a group of people considers desirable and acceptable (Dombeck & Wells-Moran 2006). Morals often reflect local rather than universal sensibilities, even though certain extreme negative behaviors, such as murder and various forms of abuse are, for the most part, universally despised (Dombeck & Wells-Moran 2006).

Tact: Tact refers to the ability to maintain good relations in dealing with people, being aware of and sensitive to diversity, and exercising self-control in all situations (Department of the Army 2006; "Marine Corps Leadership Traits" 2007).

Technical proficiency: Technical proficiency refers to "knowledge of the military sciences and skill in their application" ("Leadership" 1980, n.p.).

Unselfishness: Unselfishness means a person avoids making himself or herself "comfortable at others' expense. Unselfishness includes exercising selfless service in putting the welfare of the nation before your own—dedication to duty" (Air Force Doctrine Document 1-1 2006; Department of the Army, 2006; "Marine Corps Leadership Traits" 2007).

Values: Strongly-held beliefs and principles by which people live and the goals toward which people aspire; the source of motivation for self-improvement (Dombeck & Wells-Moran 2006).

Assumptions

The participants in the present study were considered successful and were selected based on their accomplishments as military leaders. The first assumption was that the source of information and the information itself regarding the quality of the leadership of the participants were reliable, true, and accurate. The assumption meant that the participants may not have been successful based on personal accomplishments and leadership ability because not all military promotions are necessarily warranted. A person may be promoted and achieve success based upon other than legitimate causes such as hard work and conscientious efforts. For the present study, the assumption was that the information and the source were reliable and that the participants' success as military leaders was due primarily, if not totally, to the values they held.

Participants from all military branches were selected to obtain a sample representative of the entire population of senior enlisted military leaders. The second assumption was that the primary participants were representative of the wider population of military leaders regarding accomplishments and military leadership experience. The assumption included the notion that all military branches were similar in their regard for the importance of exemplary standards for senior enlisted members.

The legitimacy or validity of responses to interview questions cannot be controlled. A third assumption was that all participants, both primary and secondary participants, understood the confidentiality of the study and would provide honest responses to all interview questions (Murray 2008). Understanding the confidentiality of the study is crucial to the validity and reliability of the study and without full disclosure to that extent, the study results would not be useful. Aside from the claim of confidentiality, participants (as military leaders) may also be motivated to provide honest and reliable data because of their support for the objective of the research, and because they derive a sense of contributory ownership (Rabinowitz & Berkowitz 2009) in the project.

Leadership is about people, the empowerment of people and about events (Greenleaf, Spears, & Covey 2002), not exclusively about military, civilian, or business situations (Yeakey 2002). The fourth assumption was that the results of the study would be more usefully applied to a military population because the present study was concerned specifically with the successful and effective training of troops in contemporary warfare.

A fifth assumption regarding the present study was that any snowball sampling (Cooper & Schindler 2006) used to identify other secondary participants would yield legitimate participants whose perceptions were accurate and representative of most others' in the leaders' sphere of influence and circle of relationships. This assumption was made because snowball sampling relies upon the referrals of the initial contacts to increase the size of the sample because these contacts may have knowledge of others with the characteristics required by the research (Callanan 2005). In the case of the present research study, the leaders would be able to identify those who are aware of and have firsthand knowledge of his or her values and resultant leadership style and characteristics.

A final assumption was that the qualitative grounded theory design with the in-depth interview methodology would accurately assess the leadership values, quality, style, characteristics, and attributes of the participants. The assumption was made because of the particularistic nature of qualitative research (Menking 2003), which allows a deeper investigation into issues and circumstances that may be of particular interest and applicability to the study. The grounded theory design coupled with the use of in-depth interviews helped ensure that the resulting theory emerged directly from the data derived from the interviews.

Scope of the Study

The purpose of the present qualitative grounded theory research study was to explore the values that influence and guide the style and practices of successful military leaders. The scope of the study encompassed an examination of the personal and professional values of a sample group of military leaders purposively selected (Cooper & Schindler 2006; "Data Selection," n.d.; Teddlie & Yu 2007) from a broad population of senior enlisted military leaders. The special characteristics limiting the selected sample included military rank and position within the command structure of the armed forces of the United States of America. The sample was a subset of the collective population of senior enlisted military advisers to U.S. military installation and service commanders. The primary participant sample size of eight was limited to the ranking senior enlisted personnel at their respective military commands. One female and seven male primary participants were involved in the study.

Limitations

Certain limiting factors or situations present internal threats to validity, fall beyond the control of the researcher, and may affect the results of the study or the interpretation of the study results and the generalizability of the study (Baron 2009). Limitations highlight the possible errors or difficulties in interpretation pertaining to the study. Baron noted that limitations are not always apparent at the beginning of the study, but may emerge as the study progresses. Limitations are neither alibis nor excuses, but simply help the research consumer understand what the results mean, and any wider application that may exist. Only those limitations expected to have a major effect on the present study are discussed here.

Problems Limiting the Research

Small and unique samples available may cause results not to be applicable beyond the study sample (Baron 2009). The unavailability and inaccessibility of an adequate number of participants due to geographic location was a problem that was considered a limiting factor in the present study. The leaders who were the focus of the study are those holding, or having held the top enlisted military leadership billets at military installations, commands, or in the particular military branch. Because the availability or the accessibility of the participants cannot be controlled, this research was limited to only those participants who are available and accessible. There was no guarantee that the initial participants would continue to be available for the duration of this research, especially as the military leaders who were the participants in the study could at any time receive unexpected reassignment orders. Baron reported lengthy studies may cause participants originally available to be unavailable for the final stages of the research.

Qualifications That May Have Limited the Research

Another limitation involved the possible lack of candor in the participants' answers. Such dishonesty would cause the results to be inaccurate and not reflect the opinions of an adequate quantity of the selected population. The effect of the dishonesty would limit the application of the study results (Baron 2009), including the resulting suggestions depicted in the theoretical model. The application of the model would not be effective if the model is based on inaccurate, imprecise, or false premises. The present study would be considered limited by the inaccuracy of the information provided by the participants or found in the documents relied upon in the conduct of the study, as indicated in the assumptions. Although the participants were encouraged to be forthright and honest in their responses, no guarantee existed that this was the case. The research validity and reliability may be compromised or qualified by this condition.

Weaknesses Related to the Research

The present study may be broadly interpreted and applied to the entire armed forces of the United States of America, but certain training and operational procedures referred to by the participants may be restricted to his or her particular military branch, due only to differing service mandates and missions. Such weaknesses were unlikely in the present study because the study was about universal values and did not address technical matters. Any existing weaknesses in this area can be addressed by the leaders tailoring or adapting the findings to the current situation (Yeakey 2002).

Reservations Related to the Research

The purposive sampling requirement was a necessary condition that intrinsically restricted participants to a smaller number (Cooper & Schindler 2006; "Data Selection," n.d.; Teddlie & Yu 2007) because they were more likely to qualify as successful leaders. Because a relatively small number of participants hold a few unique billets within the military command structure, the experiences of the participants may not have represented the actual or similar experiences or situations of the represented population. A reservation on the use of the resulting model might be that the study was based on the experiences of the relatively small number of senior leaders, and the model may not be effective when applied by junior or subordinate leaders. This observation is not expected to affect the use of the resulting model. In fact, the restriction to this small and unique group of senior leaders could be considered a benefit as it provides the opportunity for junior leaders to learn from the experiences of successful senior leaders for present or future application.

The researcher is the primary instrument in any qualitative study (Seidman 2006). Researcher bias also can be considered a limiting factor in the collection and analysis of data. Researcher bias may unintentionally be present in the present research study because the study was focused on military leaders and was conducted by a military leader.

The Research Design and Resulting Model

Grounded theory, according to Ruane and Ramcharan (2006), is dependent upon the re-creation (or reconstruction) of logic. Although the logic may be plausible, a substantial amount of work is required to accept the findings unless reliance on the informants' meaningful behavior for interpretation is considered acceptable (Ruane & Ramcharan 2006). This consideration may translate to a research limitation relevant to the grounded theory design because the resulting theoretical model may not reveal or predict accurate social meaning. Ruane and Ramcharan revealed how this shortcoming might be overcome by using ethno-methodology as an additional/triangulating approach. Their study showed how working through a case study example, informants' values and meaningful behavior can be accessed using specialized (membership category) analysis.

Another issue that may have limited this research and the use of the resulting model is a recognized limitation of the grounded theory design itself. Because of the extensive amount of time normally required to conduct a study using this design, attempts to analyze the data using any systematic, in-depth analytical procedures are often avoided. Thus, the grounded theory design can result in mere descriptions as opposed to detailed analysis needed when formulating conclusions. Without a step-by-step explanation of how the offered theoretical insights were developed, research consumers cannot truly be certain of the credibility and reliability of their source.

Delimitations

Delimitations refer to the ability to generalize the results of a study beyond the investigation parameters or outside of the study population and include factors over which there is some control (Baron 2009). The present study was structured to focus only on values, characteristics, attributes, morals, ethics, and virtues of a relatively small sample of military leaders (representative of the wider set of successful military leaders) and on perceptions of others regarding the leaders. The study sample was selective and purposive, based on extensive successful leadership experience and exemplary military service of the leaders, and the necessity of selecting other participants who were familiar with the leader (Cooper & Schindler 2006; "Data Selection," n.d.; Teddlie & Yu 2007). These issues presented delimiting factors in that they can be controlled (Creswell 2007). The generalizability and transferability of the study as well as the applicability of the resulting model may be limited to use within the military leadership population.

Generalizability of the Study

A fundamental weakness of qualitative studies is that they often have limited generalizability to a large population (Cooper & Schindler 2006) because the limitations and delimitations of a study may affect the generalizability of the study (Baron 2009). Generalizability and transferability of the results of the present study and the applicability of the resulting model might conceivably be limited to the specific military population (senior enlisted military leaders), but may also be applicable to junior enlisted leaders or the military officer corps. Although limitations and delimitations exist, the general application of the present study to all military leadership situations is not expected to be affected. Situational (or adaptive) leadership, which include transformational and transactional styles, are increasingly necessary at all echelons in the complexities of the 21st century military (Yeakey 2002).

Leadership is about people and the empowerment of people (Greenleaf et al. 2002). Because of the connection with people, leadership is neither necessarily nor entirely situation- or population-specific and may have a wide application and interpretation extending to most organizational, cultural, and personal leadership scenarios. The focus of the present study was on the exploration of personal and professional values that contribute specifically to successful military leadership. The goal was to build a theoretical model that identifies and explains those values and the effect they have on military leaders' style and practices.

The generalizability of the present study beyond the Western culture and modern civilization may be limited, based only on the types of values revealed or the population to which the values are applied. Values may be divided into two basic groups: practical values and universal values

(Recovery Nation 2009). Practical values are those values applied on a day-to-day basis to effect and manage change and that can be managed by personal interaction with other people. Universal values are the central core values that all modern societies embrace, including creativity, rationality, a quest for truth, adherence to behavioral codes, and constructive subversiveness, among other such values ("Scientific Observations" 2008).

Different cultural groups, organizations, and segments of society and the professional world vary in their perceptions of the most important practical values contributing to successful leadership. Universal values such as honesty, tolerance for diversity, and equitable treatment go beyond organizational, cultural, or societal perceptions and hinge upon universal principles and norms such as fairness, justice, and respect for others (Recovery Nation 2009). Such values as revealed by the study have a broader application and interpretation, extending to a larger segment of the human population.

Summary

The state of 21st century world affairs, including the unprecedented terrorist attack on the United States and other countries leveled by al-Qa'ida, prompted discussion and consideration of the preparation and the readiness of American fighting forces to meet the leadership challenges of the Global War on Terror (GWOT) (Toner 2006; Francis 2008; Parrish 2006). The present study was set against the backdrop of contemporary military conflicts arising out of global terrorist threats and activity. The problem in the present study was the lack of credible, qualified leaders to respond adequately to the training and leadership demands of a 21st century military (Defense and the National Interest 2007). The need to respond effectively and appropriately to these challenges with 21st century counterinsurgency measures is also an important consideration for military leaders (Peters 2007; Toner 2006).

Many of the challenges have been produced by the unprecedented and keen awareness of the American people concerning foreign perceptions of America and the American military (Huddy et al. 2005).

The contemporary demand for political correctness, even on the battlefield in the fog of war, has the effect of disadvantaging the military, placing it in a precariously and inherently dangerous position with unfortunate consequences (Swiatek 2005). Ultimately, recruiting and training a military force with the capability to meet and overcome such challenges means first acquiring capable, skilled, and experienced transformational leadership. Leadership ethics and morals, as well as the legitimacy and credibility of leadership, are concepts that inform and shape a solid foundation for transformational leadership in the 21st century military (Secretary of the Army 2006).

The purpose of the present qualitative grounded theory research was to create a model based on the exploration of the values that guide and influence the style and practices of successful military leaders. The study was designed to explore ways in which the leaders' values, virtues, ethics, and attributes might influence and inform the practice of other leaders in the military. The questions and the investigation revolved around the particular characteristics, traits, theories, practices, and specific actions of those entrusted with the training, development, and leadership of an experientially unique military force.

The study was intended to be significant in that it was designed to reveal the specific characteristics, values, and actions proven successful in military leadership scenarios. The primary use of in-depth interviews that explored specific examples for guidance and emulation was expected to accomplish this goal. Qualitative studies rely on exploration of the personal experiences of the subjects to reveal answers to the research questions (Creswell 2007). The subjective process was intended to guide the research, allowing the subject free rein in sharing significant convictions, motives, and leadership values.

Several contemporary issues formed the conceptual and theoretical framework for the present study. Awareness and understanding of these issues facilitated a more thorough conceptualization of the need for and significance of the study. Some of the issues included leadership and retention rate, leadership styles, female leadership in the military, leadership ethics, and leadership reporting issues. Each issue was imbedded in the general leadership landscape and dialogue, with a bearing on military leadership perception and quality.

Despite the assumptions and delimitations of the study, the results were expected to reveal information useful to military leaders as they face the challenge of leading a 21st century military force. Chapter 1 introduced the study and provided a foundation emerging from the background of the military leadership issues pertinent to the GWOT. Chapter 1 also presented an overview of the study. Some of the literature sources contributing to this research effort are reviewed in chapter 2.

CHAPTER 2: REVIEW OF THE LITERATURE

The contemporary political, social, and military atmosphere indicates a profound need for military leaders of character whose practices are guided by sound principles, values, and beliefs (Pfaff 2002). The purpose of the present qualitative grounded theory research was to create a model based on the exploration of the values that guide and influence the style and practices of successful military leaders. The goal was to articulate the theory integrating the necessary values, qualities, and actions of a successful leader in the 21st century military.

Chapter 1 included an introduction to the topic of this research study, the background, the problem and purpose statements, the research questions, the significance of the study, the theoretical framework, limitations of the study, and other foundational aspects. Because little is learned from repeating existing studies, a review of the available literature must first be conducted to determine what is already known about the topic of study (Leedy & Ormrod 2005). A literature review reveals the literature that already exists and what is already known about the topic.

Chapter 2 presents a discussion of how the literature review was conducted, including (a) documentation of title searches, articles, research documents, and journals researched; (b) gaps in the literature; (c) historical overview; (d) current findings and contributions to 21st century military leadership; (e) the scope of the literature review on leadership styles, characteristics, and traits; (f) review of the literature within the context of the study; and (g) conclusions emerging from the literature review.

Documentation

Of the more than 5,000 new business titles produced by the publishing industry in the United States each year, a vast majority is on leadership and various topics related to leadership (Crossan & Mazutis 2007). As suggested by Cone and Foster (2005), the ensuing literature research took the form of written and electronic books, book chapters, papers, articles, journals, and other published material. The literature review results from a systematic and logical research, analysis, and appraisal of a substantial number of these sources, as prescribed by Blum and Muirhead (2005). This section includes a discussion of two primary topics related to the conduct of the literature review. The first topic includes the sources: the title searches, articles and books, research documents, and journals, and the second involves the search methods used to locate relevant literature.

Title searches were conducted to locate scholarly and peer-reviewed electronic and printed articles and books, research documents, and journals on leadership theorists and theories. Some of the keywords and phrases used in the title search included *leadership, military leadership; leadership styles; military history; military leaders; world's greatest military leaders, Global War on Terrorism; and 21st century military*. A review of the literature concerning the various approaches to military leadership and management associated with various assumptions and theories was included in the search. These works mainly represent the writings of prominent theorists in the leadership field.

A substantial quantity of articles and books written by senior military personnel from all four branches of the U.S. military were located by using title searches. Many of the authors officially represent the various military war colleges, universities, academies, and military commands. Some contemporary and emerging military leaders, scholars, and educators, such as Abrashoff, T. J. Carlson, Dodd, Estes, McMichael, and many others, were located using title searches. Title searches also revealed some non-military sources, including works by Greenlee, Bass, Covey, Drucker, and other key authors and theorists. The title search revealed many journal articles that were applicable to the present study as well as official Pentagon reports approved for public release that addressed the subject matter.

Search Methods Used to Locate Relevant Literature

Methods of locating the sources revealed in the literature review are documented in this section. Computerized literature searches, institutional online libraries, and Web search engines using keywords, phrases, or search terms were employed in locating relevant literary information addressing the topic of the present study. This section discusses six methods used to locate relevant literature: (a) researching key authors and journals in the field of leadership and military leadership, (b) reviewing bibliographic reference sources, and (c) reviewing scholarly and academic articles. The final three methods included (d) corresponding with key contributors in the leadership field; (e) reviewing overlapping literature from other disciplines; and (f) scanning tables of contents, bibliographies, and reference lists of key journals and published academic writings and research material (Cone & Foster 2005).

Key Authors and Journals in Leadership and Military Leadership

Some of the researched leadership journals included the Academy of Strategic and Organizational Leadership Journal (ASOLJ), Leadership in Action, Leader to Leader, Leadership Quarterly, Wall Street Journal, and others. Substantial theoretical contributions to this work came from literature by key and renowned authors in the field of leadership. These included Bass, Covey, Ducker, Maxwell, Kouzes & Posner, Bartolome, Greenleaf, and notable professional military writers and biographers such as Estees, Pfaff, Swiatek, and Yeakey.

Bibliographic Reference Sources

Bibliographies and reference pages from articles, books, and journals contained potential sources for numerous other references pertaining to leadership and military leadership. The Leader to Leader Institute, originally established as the Peter F. Drucker Foundation for Nonprofit Management (Leader to Leader Institute 2007) publishes a quarterly journal that offers relevant thinking on leadership, management, and strategy by prominent leadership and management theorists. This organization provides an online reference list containing hyperlinks to each article and a list of columns published in the *Leader to Leader Journal* from 1996 forward, each linked to complete text articles.

The U.S. Army War College Department of Command Leadership and Management (DCLM) Web site includes a Web page that features work by DCLM current and former faculty members. A helpful feature of the Web page is its annotated bibliography format that includes brief summaries of each article's contents. Arizona State University, West Campus, also publishes an exhaustive A–Z online bibliography of military leadership.

Scholarly and Academic Sources

Many scholarly and academic sources were helpful in completing this research. Research papers, theses, and dissertations from colleges and universities; the U.S. Army Research Institute; U. S. Army War College; the U. S. Naval Post Graduate School; and other military institutions contributed information on military training and warrior ethos, leadership development, and military virtues, values, and morals. A search of online academic institutional library resources resulted in many scholarly resources that contributed to the present study.

Correspondence with key and reputable contributors to the field. Telephonic and written correspondence with key and reputable writers in the field of leadership revealed several sources that address the topic of this effort. These communications included correspondence with key academic leadership personnel. Correspondence with the Robert Greenleaf Center for Servant Leadership and Temple University department chairpersons for the department of human resources management revealed helpful information pertaining to the topic of the research.

Overlapping literature. Literature from the disciplines of religion and business addressed qualities and characteristics of effective followers. In the context of religion, scripture demands exemplary followership and, in many cases, demands this above aspiration to leadership.

Many biblical passages form the basis for the servant leadership concept that stresses the leader's service to the follower, as opposed to the follower's service to the leader. Scripture calls on wives to submit themselves to their husbands and suggests that husbands follow the example of Christ in giving himself for the church (Ephesians, Chap. 5). Clayton (2005) noted that in the Christian faith community, development of Christ-like character is the obvious goal of leadership development, which requires that Christian leaders take on the qualities and the character of Christ, emphasizing attitudes of selflessness, giving, and caring.

The shepherding style of leadership, also biblically founded, characterizes leaders not only as selfless, giving, and caring, but also as quick and agile thinkers, able to think ahead for the good and welfare of subordinates (McCormick & Davenport 2003). In the Old Testament of the Bible, God refers to the Israelite leaders as shepherds. In the New Testament, Christ Himself provides a shepherd-like leadership model for God's people. Peter referred to Christ as *"the Shepherd and Overseer of your souls,"* (1 Peter 2:25) and Christ called Himself the "Good Shepherd" (John 10:11). Starling (2009) noted that when leaders adopt this style of leadership, they foster a more willing and non-rebellious following.

In the world of business, Ready (2005) advocated that leadership be seen less as a list of traits and competencies and more as an effectual leader-follower relationship. Ready stressed the critical importance of followership to successful leadership, citing two reasons for leadership failure that pertain to followership and how the leader perceives and deals with followers. The first reason is an insufficient mass of critical followership, and the second reason: a poor capacity for listening by the leader.

Table of contents, bibliographies, and reference lists. Scanning the tables of contents, bibliographies, and reference lists of several major articles and books resulted in helpful sources from which emerged useful information. Scanning these sources saved research time by providing an initial indication of the publication's likelihood of containing information helpful to the present study. Both a lucid and a logical contextual overview of the contents of the publications resulted from this effort.

Literature applicable to the research concerning the population and the sample was primarily restricted to that regarding both historic and contemporary exemplary leadership examples. A review of the literature about the values that influence and guide the practices of exemplary military leaders was found mainly in the form of biographies, autobiographies, personality profiles, and historical accounts of the actions of famous leaders past and present. Some examples are *Alexander The Great's Art of Strategy: The Timeless Leadership Lessons of History's Greatest Empire Builder* by Partha Bose, *My American Journey: An Autobiography* by Colin Powell, *Profiles in Leadership* by Alan Axelrod, *For God and Glory* by Joel Hayward, *The Book of War: The Art of War* by Sun-Tzu, *Great Captains Unveiled* by B. H. Liddel Hart, *The Challenge of Command* by Roger H. Nye, *The Military 100: A Ranking of the Most Influential Leaders of All Time* by Michael Lanning, and *It's Your Ship* by Michael Abrashoff.

The vast body of literary works and available accounts of personal leadership revealed the makings of exemplary, efficient, and exceptional leaders and leadership styles. These writings concerned military leadership situations in garrison, during peacetime, and on the battlefield. Each contributed to the body of literature concerning the population and the sample and provided a historical and contemporary look at military leadership and leadership styles.

Gaps in the Literature

Three research challenges representing gaps in the literature were encountered during the literature review. The first and most significant gap in the literature on the topic of the present study was the lack of literature specifically regarding military leadership from the standpoint of 21st century warfare challenges. During the literature review, little was available regarding specific values that contribute to successful military leadership in the 21st century. Another deficiency in the available literature concerned the lack of a theory-based ethic that was clearly articulated as the focus of leadership behavior. Finally, the literature on the topic of spirituality in leadership and in the workplace was substantial, but may lack academic rigor as noted.

Historical Overview of Leadership

A brief discussion on the relevance and significance of historic military leadership to contemporary leadership and leadership studies is presented. A few cited examples of renowned leaders of the past and a brief discussion on positive vs. negative leaders (Popper, Amit, Gal, Mishkal-Sinai, & Lisak 2007) are provided. The main topics comprising this historical overview of leadership included (a) classical era leadership examples and (b) modernist era leadership examples.

Creative problem-solving skills and the ability to produce innovative solutions to the complex and nebulous challenges inherent in dynamic operational environments represent essential cognitive attributes for military leaders (Drew 2005). The importance of military leadership is sustained in the notion that throughout history, societies fortunate enough to have exemplary, creative, and innovative military leaders among their numbers have prospered and sustained themselves, whereas those without such leaders have been exploited, subjugated, or even annihilated (Province 2008). The importance of studying, analyzing, and understanding historical leadership styles and the challenges faced by historic leaders is that such study shapes the way military leaders and decision makers perceive contemporary military leadership conflicts and challenges (Kagan 2006). According to Wren, studying the past contributes to a more lucent, coherent, and cogent picture of the present, and "without knowledge of history, individuals have only their limited experiences as a basis for thought and action" (Wren 2005, p. 4).

Province (2008) asserted that the most influential leaders in world history were not produced by the church, the governments, or the scholastic centers of the world. They were produced by the military. These influential men and women represent some of the most recognized and significant forces for effective leadership the world has known. These include classical and modernist era and contemporary leaders. Their historic military leadership styles and actions could serve as inspiration for 21st century military leaders.

Many leaders are considered renowned and are legendary merely due to the magnitude of their actions. Some such leaders are not considered apt role models for the purpose of the present study due to the nature of their actions. A distinction should be made between negative and "personalized leaders" (Hitler, for example), and positive, or "socialized leaders" (Gandhi, for example) (Popper et al. 2007, p. 1). For this reason, only those positive influential military leaders will be included in the study as exemplary examples.

Classical Era Military Leadership Examples: Ancient–1700
Literary works provide information on many classical era leadership figures who exhibited qualities of successful influential leaders. Nordstrom (2004) substantially chronicled the successful military leadership career of Gustavus Adolphus (1594-1632), a Swedish king and military leader who, at the age of 17, succeeded his father to the throne. Several biographies have been produced on the life and leadership of Alexander the Great (356–323 B.C.). These include accounts by Fildes and Fletcher (*Alexander the Great: Son of the Gods*) and Hammond (*Alexander the Great: King, Commander, and Statesman*). McGill (2009) and Wolpert (2006) noted that many people considered Alexander the Great one of the brightest military minds in history. The Oliver Cromwell Association (2005) followed the life and military career of notorious statesman and military leader Oliver Cromwell (1599-1658). The literature portrays him as a spiritual and humble, yet brilliant military leader with an innovative mind.

Historical female military leaders are also worthy of note and well-chronicled in the literature (e.g., Joan of Arc, the biblical character Deborah, and Queen Amina). Williamson (2005) and Pernoud (2003) described the life, leadership, and short career of Joan of Arc (1412-1431) who, at the age of 17, proved herself as capable as the next military hero. Joan exhibited the qualities of bravery, determination, commitment, spirituality, and faith, the latter of which may have contributed to her spirit of humility. According to Judges (Chap. 4 & 5), Deborah, a prophetess, judge, and military leader who led Barak to victory against the Canaanites, demonstrated humility in relinquishing the honor for the victory to another woman Jael. Deborah was the only woman to hold the office of Judge of Israel, assuming the title and position when no men were willing to do so. "Queen Amina (1533-1610?) succeeded her mother, Bakwa Turunku in leadership of the northern Nigerian Hausa city-state of Zaria" (Patzer 2008; "Women Rulers" 2007, 1, section 11), eventually amassing numerous city-states under her control and opening trade routes that tremendously enriched Zaria's economy ("Feminism: Africa and African Diaspora" 2005).

Modernist Era Military Leadership Examples (1750–1960)
Boje and Dennehy (1999) described leaders of this era as forceful, swashbuckling types: "Authoritarian leaders who ruled their organizations with a controlling hand" (n.p.). The military leadership careers of the two Civil War contemporaries, Robert E. Lee and Ulysses S. Grant, and the American Army General George Patton are merely three examples of disparate but relevant leadership styles and personalities chronicled by Connery (2009), Petrauskaite, (2008), Campbell (2007), and the Ulysses S. Grant Homepage (2006). Theodore Roosevelt, 26th United States president, overcame a childhood fraught with illnesses and would eventually drop out of law school to begin a political leadership career (Kelly 2010). Among the leaders of this era was also a well-renowned female leader Florence Nightingale, born to wealthy land owners in 1820 (Citizendium 2009). Florence brought a certain moral character to the concept of military medical care during her time of service to the military in the Crimean war (Bloy 2009).

Current Findings in 21st Century Military Leadership

Each of these following topics bears significant impact on the ability and the effectiveness of 21st century military leaders. The topics include (a) military leadership quality; (b) the media and military leadership; and (c) ethics, values, and morals, and military leadership. Additional topics are discussed: (d) leadership convictions and the politics of war; (e) implications for the study context; and (f) individual contemporary leadership contributions.

Military Leadership Quality

The Defense and the National Interest Web site (2007) published a short article on leadership and a forum for discussion on the declining quality of military leadership over the past decade. The article mentioned complaints over the pervasiveness in the Non-Commissioned Officer (NCO) ranks of the pursuit of personal interests, to the detriment of the troops' welfare, training, and readiness. Forum participants discussed such topics as the need for mentoring juniors and for raising military standards—the type of concerns the present study was designed to address. An executive summary by Vandergriff (2006) was linked to this source; it discussed the importance of military leadership adaptability.

The Media and Military Leadership

Pasquarett (2003) discussed the joint experience of the media and the military during Operation Iraqi Freedom and the impact of media embeds on military leadership. Some of the aspects of this program discussed in the article were lessons learned, such as how well the program worked, what procedures and tactics were successful, which were unsuccessful, and recommendations for future operations to achieve a more informative program for the American public. According to Lehman (2004), effectively employed embeds can be an extremely valuable tool to an operational commander in gaining American public support and in countering enemy propaganda.

In treating the controversial topic of media misreporting of military leadership actions and decisions, Dodd (2004) took a different attitude. The article by Dodd contained a potential application to the concept of military loyalty. Dodd stated that many journalists write about military leadership from a position of ignorance. As a result, many Americans who rely upon the media sources for news about military operations receive inaccurate and unfounded reports. Dodd believed the result is a distorted and often negative portrayal of military services and military personnel.

Lehman (2004) concurred with the assessments made by Dodd, positing that when properly employed and cautiously treated, embedded media can yield favorable results for minimal investment. Failure to take the proper precautions and actions may result in negative and detrimental press coverage that eventually affects the accomplishment of military objectives (Dodd 2004; Lehman 2004). Military leaders need to manage the intake of such reporting for troops so that they respond in a calm and unwavering fashion, emerging unscathed with their service loyalty and good conduct intact.

Ethics, Morals, Values, and Military Leadership

Ethics. Pfaff (2002) addressed the concept of ethical decision making, the inevitability of confronting such issues, and choosing the most favorable means of resolving the ethical dilemmas confronting all military leaders at one time or another. Pfaff dwelled upon the ability and willingness of the leader to make ethical decisions in the face of personal and professional conflict. The conflict often arises when the leader tries to balance the demands of moral and professional concerns. Maintaining this delicate balance can sometimes translate to the difference between effective and non-effective leadership, revealed either in the outcome of the leader's actions or in the perceptions of observing followers. Pfaff noted an important consideration is the question of whether or not a leader should lay down personal morals and convictions to affect professional outcomes and advantages related to mission accomplishment.

A concise but detailed overview of the three kinds of ethics theory and the role of ethics theory in the decision-making process for the military leader was provided by Pfaff (2002). The three kinds of theory are described as utilitarianism, rules-based systems, and virtue ethics (Pfaff 2002). The role of theory is to provide an approach or a coherent framework that helps leaders consider the reasoning behind the actions they take (or those they require their subordinates to take) and sort the good and bad reasons for the actions (Pfaff 2002).

Leaders ought to be aware of the difficulties that accompany theory choice because the theoretical foundation for determining right or wrong may be different from one theory to the next (Pfaff 2002). Theories may predicate right or wrong by virtue of consequences—utilitarianism/"consequentialism" (Brown 2001, p. 1). The utilitarian theory asserts that the action is right as long as the best consequences result (e.g., happiness is maximized) (Brown 2001).

Theories also predicate right or wrong, depending upon whether or not the action conforms to a moral rule or principle in accordance with Kantian ethics or deontology (Brown 2001; Pfaff 2002). Moral rules are those required by rationality (Brown 2001). In contrast with utilitarian or consequential theories, deontological theories do not judge the morality of an action based on the resulting state of affairs, but rather on conformity to moral norms which must be obeyed, regardless of the consequences (Stanford Encyclopedia of Philosophy 2007).

The virtue theory—Aristotle's moral theory—regards an action as right if a virtuous person would perform it in similar circumstances (Brown 2002). Hence, right or wrong is predicated on the character of the person committing the act (Pfaff 2002). A virtuous person acts virtuously, or exercises virtue — a trait required to flourish as a human being (Brown, 2001).

According to Pfaff (2002), reliance on any one theory alone may be inadequate for ethical decision making. Pfaff advocated reliance on a number of techniques that consider moral principles, consequences, and character. Considering the consequences and dilemmas military leaders face in choosing actions resulting from any theory choice, Pfaff advocated the theory of virtue ethics because of its moral foundations. The virtue ethics theory avoids most dilemmas because the focus does not involve deciding between two negative outcomes or between conflicting rules (Pfaff 2002). Virtue ethics focuses on the character of the leader and his or her propensity to do what is right. This is especially needful amidst the complications and heightened dynamics of contemporary warfare (Pfaff 2002).

Morals. Much has been written and much conversation has taken place on the topic of morals and the military. The literature review revealed some sources that commend the military and its observance of and adherence to traditional American and societal morals. Other sources reveal blatant and unscrupulous moral indiscretions committed by some members of the military, whether they are claimed to be isolated or commonplace. It might be noted that a random review of the literature revealed more negative sentiments than positive ones regarding military morals. Perhaps this bias may be a reflection of the more liberal-minded tendencies of contemporary society as opposed to traditional conservative tendencies.

Values. Values are the foundation, the cornerstone, and the heart of one's character (MCWP 6-11 2002). People are defined by the values they hold because values constantly guide their decisions, conduct, and behavior (MCWP6 11). Military values are important because the military is responsible not only to society but also to its own mission to set and adhere to a high moral code (Rice 2010). The military value system, asserted Rice (2010), can provide a healthy value system model for contemporary society, considering the recent falling away of traditional societal values. Military laws and the Uniform Code of Military Justice (UCMJ) form the foundation and source of the military value system (Rice 2010). As Rice noted, the nature of military leadership to promote virtuous behavior is based on a traditional value system in meeting and withstanding detrimental contemporary social trends.

People with military experience possess discernible, yet intangible qualities and traits that seem to exist for the most part across all branches of the military (Rice 2010). These qualities and traits are exemplified in the core values of each military service. For example, the Navy and Marine Corps core values of honor, courage, and commitment produce disciplined men and women of character, confidence, and strong team-building skills, responsible and accountable for their actions (Rice 3020) and those of their subordinates.

Kincaid (2004) wrote about moral corruption in the military, citing Dr. Herbert London's analysis in which he discussed the relationship between moral strength and military might. Kincaid suggested that even amid the scandals that erupted during the Iraq war and the embarrassment that ensued, the moral good accomplished by the vast majority of the troops can be neither overlooked nor denied. Kincaid wrote then that should the Iraqi liberation effort fail, it might be seen as the result of media sensationalism which exploited the indiscretions of a few soldiers who have been exploited by western culture. Many people rate the level of morals in American society as less than good, blaming the moral decline on lack of media proficiency and failure to combat the indiscretions rather than exploit them (Kincaid 2004).

Ibrahim (2008) took a more critical view of military morals, implying that many in the military would react with violence (weapons) before taking the time to reason. Ibrahim further attacked military morals in his criticism of Marine General and former Chairman of the Joint Chiefs of Staff Peter Pace's strong stance against homosexuality and gays and lesbians serving in the military. Those on the other side of this controversy point to Pace's position as a morally right one, stating that the United States would not be well-served to adopt a policy condoning such immorality (Ibrahim 2008). Those on each side of the controversy consider themselves to be upholding moral principles and conduct when taking such opposing stances.

The infamous military scandal involving severe indiscretions that took place at the Abu Graib prison in Iraq is often cited (among others) as proof of the immorality of the U.S. Military. Based on such claims, unofficial charges were lodged against the then sitting administration by some people (Carter 2004). Despite the fact that such incidents did occur, the overall U.S. military morals ethos and framework is nevertheless altruistic (Micewski 2008) and worthy of credit. The ethos of the United States military is undeniably focused on the collective good of society, even though the individual soldier faces the possibility of physical sacrifice daily as the outcome of his or her engagement (Micewski 2008). Finally, social science research indicated the U.S. military has clearly accomplished more in terms of racial equality and the redressing of racial wrongs than any other societal segment of the American population.

Leadership Conviction and the Politics of War
Torr (2005) described the Bush administration's stance concerning nations that posed a threat to the United States of America with respect to terrorism, commonly referred to as the Bush doctrine. Torr clearly revealed the leadership position and conviction of this presidential

leader. President Bush's position concerning the possibility of preemptive war against what he classified as rogue nations was presented. Despite harsh critics of the "Bush doctrine of preemption" (Torr, n.p.), President Bush maintained his leadership conviction that, when necessary, a nation must not hesitate to employ such tactics in the interest of national security and the security of American allies. The implications arising from this article made it clear that sometimes leaders must face the inevitable challenge of exercising the courage of conviction in opposing popular opinion.

Implications for the Study Context

Military leaders study and practice ethical principles to support and confirm their personal value system and guide their moral behavior (Krulak 2000). As outlined in chapter 1, mere mission accomplishment often is insufficient to satisfy those to whom the military is ultimately accountable and who exercise unprecedented scrutiny of military ac tions (Gerges 2004, Helm 2006; Rivkin 2004). A logical conclusion is that the intense and increased scrutiny of American defense forces, both domestically and internationally, has resulted in the need for ethical, uncompromising, and effective leadership in the 21st century more than at any other time in American history. Uncompromising leadership often means standing up to opposition on and off the battlefield.

Because intentionally harming or killing innocent people is not morally acceptable, military members must demonstrate the capacity to exercise compassion, integrity, morality, and decency, while accomplishing the unpleasant task of eradicating or deterring enemies (Pfaff 2002). Acquiring and developing the caliber of leadership resulting in the instillation of virtue ethics as an ethical framework in followers have comprised a key issue in the 21st century military, according to Pfaff (2002). The practice of virtue ethics has become tantamount to the need for effectiveness and acceptability of American defense forces. According to the *Marine Corps Manual* ("Leadership" 1980), the following paragraph regarding leadership qualities was composed by Major General John A. Lejeune, 13th Commandant of the U.S.

Marine Corps. His words, which follow, were published in the *Marine Corps Manual*, 1921 edition, and illustrated the significance of effective military leadership.

Leadership. – Finally, it must be kept in mind that the American soldier responds quickly and readily to the exhibition of qualities of leadership on the part of his officers… Some of these qualities are industry, energy, initiative, determination, enthusiasm, firmness, kindness, justness, self-control, unselfishness, honor, and courage. Every officer should endeavor by all means in his power to make himself the possessor of these qualities and thereby to fit himself to be a real leader of men. (1-23)

An implication of that statement is that the mark of an effective leader is, first of all, the ability to persuade a following. Second, effective leaders also produce high quality followers through personal example. The targeted qualities to be developed in military troops as a response to the leadership styles, traits, and competencies exhibited by the leader include many of the same characteristics possessed by the leader, because the leader sets the example (Bantu-Gomez 2004; Shriberg et al. 2002).

Individual Contemporary Leadership Contributions
Emerging literary contributions in the field of leadership contributing to the present study took the form of biographies, autobiographies, books, and articles by both military and civilian leaders. These contemporary leaders and authors contributed pertinent insight into leadership in the aftermath of the GWOT. The literature provided insight into the military and political leadership experiences of many prominent contemporary leaders to include Colin Powell (retired U.S. Army general and former U.S. Secretary of State) and Rudolph Giuliani (former New York City mayor and 2008 Republican Party presidential candidate). Yeakey (2002), Major, U.S. Army Retired, shared military leadership wisdom on adaptive military leadership models, theory, and strategy. Yeakey discussed how refinement in situational leadership can benefit contemporary combat leaders. Situational leadership promotes

timely adaptation of a leader's style to the followers' professional developmental stage and to the situation at hand.

A uniquely Marine perspective to the concept of military leadership was articulated by Boardman (2002) in his book *Unforgettable Men in Unforgettable Times: Stories of Honor, Courage, Commitment, and Faith from World War II*. Boardman expanded on the Navy and Marine Corps core values of honor, courage, and commitment, injecting the concept of faith in God by adding the word faith. Each leadership vignette shared strengthens the character and develops the faith of military leaders and troops. General Charles C. Krulak, 31st Commandant of the United States Marine Corps, wrote the foreword to Boardman's book. Krulak related the two inextricably linked traits of character and faith to the preparation of personal spirit. Krulak, in the foreword to the book, asserted that one must develop both character and faith for complete spiritual preparation. The development of character results from the embracement of certain core values: For the Marines, these are honor, courage, and commitment. Individual development of faith, Krulak (as cited in Boardman 2002) explained, emerges as one places trust in God and is strengthened with the ability to withstand adversities.

Perhaps more useful to the present study than any literature source noted thus far was a work by one of the participants in the present study. The work proved highly valuable because it provided an in-depth and detailed look into the leader, his character, his background, and the qualities that combined to give him success as a leader. Most notable and valuable to this leadership contribution were the detailed revelations concerning the origins of this leader's successful 35-year iconic military career.

Through a series of intense and in-depth interviews, the present research study was designed to explore the values, virtues, attributes, and style that contributed to the outstanding leadership habits, contributions, and accomplishments of McMichael and other study participants. McMichael attained the highest rank to which an enlisted Marine can aspire, and also claimed the distinction as the first African American to accomplish this achievement. McMichael (2008) spoke of the roots and the values from which were honed effective leadership style, proven not just in the military but also in all walks of life. Transformational leadership qualities and values were evident in McMichael's conviction that "No one can lead without first truly caring" (p. xiii).

Most important to McMichael (2008) were the values and fundamental concepts taught by his grandmother, described as "compassion, commitment, honesty, integrity, and good old-fashioned discipline" (p. xiii). McMichael revealed 10 tried and proven successful leadership principles with anecdotal explication and examples. A valuable contribution to this research effort, McMichael's book, *Leadership: Achieving Life-Changing Success from Within*, provided a rare and candid look into the life and the making of a military leader. Leadership in social psychology deals primarily with two main considerations: how one becomes a leader, and how one becomes a good or better leader (Levine & Moreland 2006). Leadership is best understood by studying its effectiveness, characteristics and style, follower attributes, leadership behavior, and context (Nemitz-Mills 1999).

Scope of Literature Review
on Leadership Styles, Characteristics, and Traits

The literature on the subjects of leadership and military leadership ranged from biographies and autobiographies to texts and other literature developed by the military and those recommended as components to military commanders' professional reading lists. All the military service branches have developed leadership manuals that contributed substantially to the available literature on the topic. The scope of the literature review on two aspects of leadership—leadership style and leadership qualities—are reviewed in this section.

Leadership Styles

Because leadership is the one common factor in every successful organization (Shriberg et al. 2002), much has been written addressing the various styles, theories, and techniques of effective leadership. Yammarino, Dionne, Chun, and Dansereau (2005) noted at least 17 leadership theories. The theories range from classical approaches (e.g., path-goal theory) to contemporary approaches (e.g., charismatic and transformational leadership). Behavioral scientists used typology to classify leader behavior based on style as early as 1920 (Moutet 2004). Beginning in the 20th century, certain styles of leadership are more prominent and recognizable in leadership literature than are others (Shriberg et al. 2002). Although the following leadership styles are some of the more widely recognized, accepted, and adopted models, they do not present an all-inclusive list of leadership styles.

Charismatic leadership. The German sociologist Max Weber developed the charismatic leadership model in the 1920s (de Jong 2007). Weber described charismatic leadership as that based on devotion to the extraordinary, heroic, or exemplary character of the leader. Yukl (2010) pointed to charismatic leadership as the best example of how the distinct lines of research separating theories, such as trait, situational, and behavioral, have been blurred, integrating the theories into a single comprehensive concept.

Participative leadership. Participative leadership theory proposes that the ideal type of leadership takes into account the opinions and input of others using various decision procedures that afford others influence over the leader's decisions (Yukl 2010). The decision procedures used to involve other people include (a) autocratic, (b) consultation, (c) joint decision, and (d) delegation. The four procedures range on a continuum from *no influence by others* to *high influence by others* in the order depicted in Figure 1.

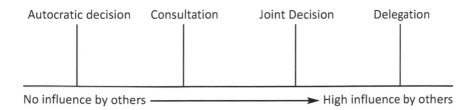

Figure 1. Decision procedures continuum. *Note.* From Leadership in Organizations (7th ed.), by G. Yukl, 2010, Upper Saddle River, NJ: Pearson Education. Adapted with permission.

Situational leadership. Often ascribed to by military leaders, situational leaders promote leaders' adaptability to particular situations and circumstances (Yeakey 2002). According to this leadership theory, no single best way to influence people exists (Kouzes & Posner 2007). Hershey and Blanchard's situational leadership theory advanced the assumption that the leader's style should be adapted to the developmental style of the followers, based on their competence and motivation (Prewitt 2004). Yeakey indicated situational leadership is particularly effective in rapidly changing and volatile combat conditions.

Transactional leadership and transformational leadership. Transactional leadership has been referred to by Bass (1999) as the process whereby an individual can influence followers through an exchange of promises or holding contingencies. Bass noted, in transactional leadership, "the leader promises rewards for acceptable performance or threats and disciplinary punishment for poor performance" (11). The concept of transformational leadership advanced by Bass (1999) clearly indicated the stark contrast between transactional and transformational leadership. According to Bass, transformational leadership refers to the leader successfully focusing the attention and the energy of the follower beyond self-interest to a higher level of "maturity and ideals" aimed at uplifting and affirming the value of "others, the organization and society" (11).

Servant leadership. Greenleaf (1991) described the servant-leader as "servant first" (7). In his words, "It begins with the natural feeling that one wants to serve, to serve *first*. Then conscience choice brings one to aspire to lead" (7). Expounding on the Greenleaf's work, Barbuto and Wheeler (2007) listed and explained the servant leader's 10 characteristics: listening, empathy, healing, awareness, persuasion, conceptualization, foresight, stewardship, commitment to growth of people, and building community. Barbuto and Wheeler also noted that the ultimate servant leader develops and continually improves upon each of these 10 characteristics.

The managerial grid. Blake and Mouton's (1985) managerial grid depicts the relationship between the manager's concern for the workers and the manager's concern for the work to be done. The concept is known as the task vs. person preference (Van Eersel 2008). The managerial grid framework depicts seven leadership styles manifested where human interaction occurs (Grid International 2009). The leadership styles are described as (a) *controlling*: the leader directs and dominates by setting a clear course of action; (b) *accommodating*: the leader often yields and complies to establish and maintain harmony; (c) *status quo*: the leader seeks balance and compromises for the sake of acceptability; (d) *indifferent*: the leader evades and alludes to avoid problems; (e) *paternalistic*: the leader will prescribe and guide by defining initiatives for everyone; (f) *opportunistic*: the leader exploits to persuade others to support results that provide private or personal benefits; and (g) *sound*: the leader encourages contribution and commitment by inviting the involvement of others (Grid International 2009).

Lewin's leadership styles. Lewin directed a study conducted by Lippitt and White (Underwood 2003). The study, known as "Leadership and Group Life," resulted in the rating of three original types of leadership models: democratic, authoritarian, and laissez-faire. Underwood reported the democratic style seems to be the most favorable, with authoritarian being second most favorable.

Other literature. Other literature concerning leadership styles and theory by renowned theorists was also available. Bolman and Deal (2008) developed four practical perspectives to assist managers in understanding their organizations. The four perspectives consisted of structural, human resources, political, and symbolic frameworks.

D. Q. Mills (2005) provided a contrast and comparison between Asian and American leadership styles. Mills concluded that differences existed between the two, and explored whether those differences were attributable to the differences between American and Asian cultures or to differing stages of corporate development within the cultures. The findings indicated that although culture does influence the way an organization functions, the developmental stage plays a more significant role. As Asian companies come to rely more on professional workers and services, Mills found they also take on a more participative and empowering style of management as opposed to the autocratic style.

Joseph (2003) researched leadership styles and emotional competencies. Joseph tested the hypothesis that "the leadership style of a manager is a function of the emotional competencies of that individual" (1). The study results supported the position that based on the empirical data connecting leadership styles and competencies, the characteristics of the leadership styles could be predicted, thus showing the hypothesis to be true.

Steward (2006) explained that James McGregor Burns first set the stage for the evolution of the concept of transformational leadership in 1978. Burns set forth two opposite types of leadership: transformational and transactional. The two are contrasted on the basis of the leader's emphasis in leading. Transactional leaders seek to manage followers by exchanging one thing for another, and they use a system of rewards to gain cooperation, according to Steward. Transformational leaders motivate followers to seek to satisfy higher needs (Bass 1990, 1996, 1999).

Tendai (2006) asserted that although styles of leadership may vary considerably, just two broad types of leadership are apparent. The styles are the authoritarian or formal type of leadership and the supportive, more flexible type of leadership. Tendai initially differentiated between *styles* and *types* of leadership. Clark (2007) posited that to be an effective leader, one must be, know, and do certain things. These are attributes acquired through conscientious hard work and study. Clark also noted that good leaders continually work to improve their education, knowledge, and skills.

Other sources included works by Bass (1996, 1999), Blake and Mouton (1985), Bolman and Deal (2008), Drucker (1967), Kouzes and Posner (2007), and Greenleaf (1977, 1991), and writings, manuals, and books produced by the leadership entities of the military services. The conduct of this research enriches and adds to the existing body of literature a perspective from a personal and experiential point of view. Real and practical citations and examples from the experiences and theories of successful leaders further enhance the study.

Leadership Qualities

Leadership theory in the Management and Leadership section of the *Marine Corps Manual* ("Leadership" 1980) stressed three important leadership qualities for Marine leaders. Leadership qualities used to describe Marine leaders are *inspiration, technical proficiency*, and *moral responsibility* ("Leadership" 1980). The leadership qualities are applicable to all military personnel, followers as well as leaders, because leaders set the example for followers (Bantu-Gomez 2004; Shriberg et al. 2002). The leadership qualities are important for followers, as followers ascribe to the guidance and the vision of their leaders and often exhibit the same leadership qualities in the achievement of their own tasks and roles (Thomas 2001).

Be, know, do. The new *Army Leadership* manual FM 22-100 lays out a dynamic framework describing its leadership principle of be, know, do (Leader to Leader Institute 2007). According to the *ArmyStudyGuide* (2008), "The framework applies to leaders at any level, in any situation, just as Army values apply at all times to all soldiers" (n.p.). The be, know, do principle asserts that the Army leader who demonstrates competence and character will act to attain excellence by being, knowing, and doing certain things (*ArmyStudyGuide* 2008).

Be represents what the soldier must be and points to the values of loyalty, duty, respect, selfless service, honor, integrity, and personal courage, and the attributes of mental, physical, and emotional excellence. Know represents the skills required of soldiers, to include interpersonal, conceptual, technical, and tactical skills they must have. Do represents the actions of an effective leader: influencing, operating, and improving (*ArmyStudyGuide* 2008).

Leadership and followership traits. According to Moutet (2004), because of practical experience, many executives and military leaders believe that inner traits create the personal power that makes successful leaders. In leading by example, leaders aim to create in followers the same traits they themselves demonstrate as effective leaders (Bantu-Gomez 2004; Shriberg et al. 2002). Moutet cited certain traits common to executive leaders. These traits, which eventually become apparent in followers, include (a) self-confidence and emotional stability; (b) willingness to take leadership responsibility; and (c) competence in facing and handling new situations. Other traits include (d) warmth, sensitivity, and sympathy; (e) intellect, (f) dependability, consistency, and reliability; (g) ability to identify with goals and values of followers; and (h) enthusiasm and the ability to communicate well.

Concentration, focus, and goal accomplishment. Drucker (1967) wrote substantially concerning the ability of leaders to maintain focus, to concentrate, and to establish and adhere to priorities in accomplishing goals. Drucker emphasized the concept of undertaking issues one at a time. Drucker wrote, Drucker wrote, "If there is any one 'secret' of effectiveness, it is concentration. Effective executives do first things first and they do one thing at a time" (10).

Trustworthiness. Boje (2003) suggested that in the 2000s, the quest is for traits that can be trusted, and that these emanate from the origins of spiritual and servant leadership. Boje discussed in some depth the Greenleaf concept of servant leadership, but also addressed the concepts of spirituality and trust as leadership traits. Boje listed integrity, competency, consistency, loyalty, and openness as dimensions of trust.

Leadership habits. Covey (1989, 2004) delineated eight habits used by effective people, family members, and principle-centered leaders. According to Covey (1989), these people are proactive; they start with the end in mind; they prioritize; they focus on winning; they seek to understand first, then to be understood; they synergize; and they seek continuous improvement. Finally, and perhaps more importantly in the leadership arena, Covey stated they find their voice and help others do the same.

Influence. Maxwell (2007) discussed influence as the definition of leadership and setting priorities as the key to leadership. Maxwell noted that this definition goes beyond merely defining the leader to considering the leader's ability to influence followers and others outside the normal sphere of influence of the leader. One of the indicators of leadership effectiveness is follower perceptions and attitudes about the leader (Yukl 2010). Maxwell argued that this definition goes to the very character of the individual, because without integrity and trustworthiness, the leader's ability to influence is diminished.

Follower characteristics. Good followers are important because they exhibit the common characteristics that reinforce leadership (Nemitz-Mills 1999). Some important characteristics and traits of good followers include self-management; commitment to a purpose larger than themselves; professional competence; and courage, honesty, and credibility (3). Equally important, according to Latour and Rast (2004), transformational leaders value followers and show concern their professional and personal development.

Multiple Perspectives and Opposing Viewpoints on Leadership
The literature review indicated that a considerable amount of attention has been focused on the multiple perspectives and opposing viewpoints regarding leadership. The literature relating to spirituality and leadership, and spirituality and military leadership is reviewed in this subsection. Some opposing viewpoints on leadership theories are also discussed in this section.

Spirituality and leadership. Spirituality is emerging as a prominent issue in the culture of organizational leadership and in the workplace (Fry & Matherly 2007). Fawcett, Brau, Rhoads, Whitlark, and Fawcett (2008) cited affirmation, belonging, and competence (described as aspects of spirituality) as critical to inspiring organizational cultures. According to Varughese (2008), more recently, leadership styles, values, and principles typically emerge from the world's spiritual or religious contexts and foundations, whether of Christian or other religious persuasions.

Servant leadership is a prime example of this concept, as the values stressed by the servant leader appear overwhelmingly biblical in context. In the Bible, Jesus clearly portrayed the role of a servant when He washed the feet of His disciples (St. John 13: 4-5). Varughese (2008) posited that servant leadership is an "ancient concept, tried, tested, and vested with the authority of the world's spiritual and religious texts" and "is slowly rising to the surface in today's turbulent times" (n.p.). Greenleaf (1977) advanced the modern concept of servant leadership, asserting that only followers can grant true authority worthy of allegiance. True authority, according to Greenleaf (1977), occurs in response to the leader's servant nature.

According to Dent, Higgins, and Wharff (2005), the way in which religion and spirituality relate to organizational leadership has become an important issue for management practitioners and researchers. Organizations with workplace spirituality programs not only bestow benefits to the individual worker but also create organization-wide benefits in terms of increased productivity, diminished attrition, and reduced absenteeism (Fry & Matherly 2007). A large portion of the literature regarding the issue is found not in academic, but in general publications and may be considered less rigorous (Dent et al. 2005).

According to Parmley (2005), *Sharpe's Handbook of Workplace Spirituality and Organizational Performance* supported an integrated and objectively definable approach to spirituality in the workplace. E-mail correspondence with Giacalone and Benefiel (August 4, 2007), editors of Parmley's book, revealed an additional source—Fry's work on spiritual leadership—which Giacalone indicated may be accessed in the *Leadership Quarterly* and a number of books on the subject. A Web-based search revealed a number of resources by Fry. Fry (2007) described spirituality in the workplace as the "key to high performance and effectiveness in the 21st century" (2007, n.p.). Much of Fry's works on the topic of workplace spirituality proved to be beneficial to the current study.

Spirituality and military leadership. Although considerable information existed with regard to spirituality in the workplace, the concept as it pertained to a military context was less extensive, as reflected in the literature review. W. Smith (2007) contended that military service in itself is something akin to a religious experience, especially in combat arms. American soldiers tend to grasp and appreciate the values of religious and spiritual virtues implicitly, despite the political and professional push for separation of church and state (Smith, W. 2007).

A rigorous and intense debate in civilian professional and political arenas concerns the constitutional intent regarding the concept of separation of church and state (Price 2004). According to Greenslit (2006), recent ethical dilemmas have arisen in the military over personal religious expression. While military academies and schools tended to maintain a somewhat traditional connection between spirituality and the workplace, the environment in those institutions has begun to change. Parco and Fagin (2007) discussed at length some of the issues of intolerance pertaining to spirituality and the military as they existed at the U.S. Air Force and other military academies, concluding with suggestions about how military leaders should address the issue of evangelism in the military.

Trait and behavior theories. Diverse perspectives and opposing viewpoints are represented by the works of theorists and philosophers of the various schools of leadership. Perhaps the most important among the opposing viewpoints has to do with the position taken by behavioral theorists and their points of emphasis as opposed to that taken by the trait theorists (Moutet 2004). According to Moutet (2004), trait theorists searched for those traits universally associated with effective leadership, whereas behaviorists were interested in one best leadership style.

Other leadership theories addressed in the literature included contingency theory (Fiedler 1967) and situational theory (Hershey & Blanchard 1969). Prewitt (2004), in discussing the theory of situational leadership, noted that different situations or scenarios call for different responses and different skills. Prewitt noted that what works in one situation might not work in another.

Military Leadership and the Social
and Political Context of the Study

The scope of the literature on military leadership involved (a) military leadership styles and (b) virtue ethics and military leadership. Clear definitions of the contextual factors in which 21st century military leaders operate were developed. These included the political and social environments surrounding the Global War on Terrorism. The goal was to discover the relevant existing literature with regard to each of these factors, the sample group, the study environment, and the leadership setting.

Military leadership styles

Because leadership involves the most basic of human behaviors (e.g. emotions and motivations), leadership may be explored in many different organizational settings and types (Schriberg et al. 2002). The military environment provides one of the best contexts for studying leadership, and has gradually come to the forefront of leadership forums and discussions. This part of the literature review concerns the literature about leadership styles most often used by military leaders. The literature review revealed that substantial studies and discussions revolve around the concept of heroism, with the aim of discovering what goes into the making of a military leader—a hero. Some of the leadership styles often identified with the military are (a) transactional and transformational (Bass 1996); (b) combat leadership (Ballard 2005); (c) authoritative, participative, and delegative (Clark 2008); and (d) situational (Yeakey 2002).

Transactional and Transformational Leadership

Willenz (2003) discussed the implications of transformational and transactional leadership for army troop leadership. One study found that the practice of combining performance rewards with building mission-specific identification provides good indictors of simulated unit performances in highly stressful and uncertain times and situations. Bass (1996) argued that the dominance of transactional leadership approaches in the military, the educational, and the industrial arenas is currently challenged due to an evolution of values and expectations in the workplace. Research by Bass, Avolio, Jung, and Berson (2003) studied leadership ratings from units operating in stable conditions and explored how they might predict future performance of the same units under stressful and uncertain conditions.

Combat Leadership

Ballard (2005) studied the diaries and letters of Civil War General U.S. Grant to unveil the secrets of his military victories and the strategies and techniques he employed in commanding troops in battle. Ballard's work detailed many of General Grant's strategic and tactical concepts during the period from the Civil War to the Battle of Chattanooga in which he established his leadership position as supreme commander of the Union armies. Ballard explored the contents of Grant's diaries and letters in an effort to reveal the role of those formative war years in the production and the shaping of one of the world's most prominent military leaders.

Authoritarian, Participative, and Delegative Leadership

Three well-known styles of leadership, having the same elements described by Yukl (2010) as a continuum, are authoritarian or autocratic, participative or democratic, and delegative or free rein (Clark 2008). The authoritarian/autocratic style emphasizes the authority of the leader. The participative/democratic style emphasizes the leader's inclusion of one or more employees in decision making, with the leader as the final decision-making authority. The delegative/free rein style emphasizes employee decision making, with the leader responsible for the decisions made, as described by Clark.

Situational Leadership

The styles and approaches to leadership are wide and varied (Yammarino et al. 2005), and necessarily so because one leadership style is not likely to be effective in all situations (Shriberg et al. 2002; Yeakey 2002). Yeakey posited situational leaders adapt their style to the situation and the developmental stage or level of the follower. The style reflects the readiness and the willingness of the follower to perform assigned tasks with competence and motivation (North Georgia College and State University 2004). *The Army Leadership* field manual (FM 22100) stressed leaders should be capable of adjusting their style of leadership to the particular situation or circumstance with which they are confronted and to followers (Yeakey 2002).

Virtue Ethics and Military Leadership

Pfaff (2002) as previously mentioned discussed the requirement for military leaders to balance the demands of morality with those of the profession of arms. Pfaff asserted that military leaders facing this dilemma must consider (a) immediate and long-term goals, (b) consequences and effects the decisions will have on others in attaining the goals, and (c) the rules and principles governing the profession. When a conflict arises among these three, leaders need a way to determine the most ethical approach. Among three ethical theories (rule-centered ethics, utilitarian ethics, and virtue ethics), Pfaff concluded that virtue ethics had certain advantages over the other two, as good leadership entails more than duty and consequences. The virtue approach, according to Pfaff, allows leaders to explore and articulate this in ways the others do not.

Virtue approach. Dion (2007) described military virtues as those grounded in the traditions and customs of a nation's military services and developed throughout its history. Pfaff (2002) noted that according to Aristotle (384-322 B. C.), they reflect the way all virtues are acquired. Dion suggested traditional military virtues include loyalty; morale and physical courage; integrity, respect, and honor; and service to country. Pfaff also discussed military leadership and cross-cultural and inter-religious dialogue in ethical issues in the military services.

Sword and shield approach. C. Toner (2006) discussed the integration of the "'sword and shield' approaches into one coherent and comprehensive military ethic" (1). The "sword approach" was described by C. Toner as the dominant approach to military ethics and focused on fighting the nation's wars. The sword approach derived its ethic from the requirement imposed on soldiers through its purpose. The alternative is the "'shield approach,' which focuses on articulating a warrior code as a moral shield that can safeguard soldiers' humanity through the stresses and losses of war" (1).

Political and Social Context of the Study

The present study was conducted within the context of the 21st century political and social backdrop of the major ongoing military conflicts of the time. The conflicts include the war in Iraq, the GWOT, and the Middle East conflict. The research context in terms of each of these aspects is crucial to ascertaining the importance and relevance of the study.

Political Context

The extent of the political context of the GWOT was revealed during the 2004 presidential election campaign when politicians as well as private citizens debated the legitimacy of the war (Spencer 2007). Theisen's (2008) argument against the legitimacy of the GWOT, in which he argued that the war on terror was a war *of* terror, is an example. Much has been written concerning the politics of war and the unavoidable impact it has on military operations and troop morale (R. Kohn 2008). The literature review revealed that newspaper and journal articles by opinionated political pundits, best-selling books and documentaries, and electronic media carry play-by-play accounts of military operations from a political view. The relevance of this context to military leadership, according to R. Kohn, is that what occurs in the political arena, to include perceptions of the military, affects troop morale, which affects the effectiveness of the leadership effort.

R. Kohn (2008) adequately captured the nature of the friction between the civilian and military entities and illustrated how political opinions and actions affect military objectives and decisions and ultimately leadership efforts. According to R. Kohn, the ever-increasing politicization of the military has fostered extreme cynicism and distrust from elected political figures toward the military. Solely to avoid the public perception of not supporting the troops, friction resulting from differences in political views concerning the GWOT has been kept private.

Social Context

From a social standpoint, many people have taken sides for or against the U.S. military based solely on social (to include religious, conservative, and liberal) influences (Beatty 2007). Some writers have found ways to contest the legitimacy of war and express opposition to the military and military leadership based on racial, economic, and humanitarian issues and injustices, as noted by Beatty (2007). According to Beatty, one critical anti-war pundit asserted, "The Iraq war, like most American wars, is a poor man's fight" (1), alluding to a suggested exploitation of the vulnerability of young Americans who make up the all-volunteer army.

Other critics have argued that the military is biased and selective in releasing information concerning the opinions and viewpoints of the public regarding the war (Smith-Stark 2007). Many war observers and an overwhelming majority of the military itself stand in stark contrast to these views. Smith-Stark reported that one military leader asserted that 80–90% of the electronically posted comments to a popular cyberspace forum were in approval of the military efforts in terms of getting information about the war out to the public domain. These issues and situations represent the social context in which the current study was conducted and the typical literary treatment of the context of the study.

Conclusion

An analysis of the literature review conducted for the present study indicated that leadership and military leadership has been the focus of much academic, political, and otherwise opinionated discussion and speculation in recent years. The conclusion derived from the literature review is that no substantial deficiency of literature exists about the subject matter of leadership and military leadership, regardless of the gap in literature addressing the focused specific context of the study: to determine the values that contribute to the achievement of effective leadership for the challenges of 21st century warfare. The study is expected to add to and strengthen the resource pool and diminish the existing gap. The existing literature takes different forms and contexts.

Regarding the first research question, there have been many studies and discussions on the subject of heroism, with the goal of discovering what goes into the making of a military leader—a hero (Thomsong 2004). Few of the studies and discussions elaborated on the specific values contributing to leadership success. The literature review explored research associated with specific military leadership styles and some of the challenges of leadership, as discussed by Kouzes and Posner (2007).

The focus of Research Question 2 concerns the specific actions of military leaders in the resolution of the ethical problems they confront. A daunting challenge for military leaders is responding morally and ethically in the decisions they must make, despite possible conflicts between moral values and professional values (Dion 2007; Pfaff 2002; Toner, C. 2006). Leaders' actions and practices, as opposed to mere theory, are of critical importance (Le Pla & Roberts 2004). A serious consideration is that of whether or not a leader should abandon personal morals and convictions to affect professional outcomes and advantages related to mission accomplishment (Pfaff 2002).

Much of the literature concerned some of the challenges of leadership and presented ways in which leaders should confront and overcome the challenges (Kouzes & Posner 2007). According to Kouzes and Posner (2007), leaders must develop value-based practices and styles to enhance their ability to face and overcome the many challenges of leadership to achieve success. Transformational (Bass 1996) and servant leadership (Greenleaf 1977), although not exclusively focused on values, are two examples of values-based leadership practices and styles.

The literature review revealed a lack of sufficient theoretical models that exclusively explain successful, values-based military leadership. The majority of the literature encountered in the review concerned leadership and theoretical models in terms of identifying the competencies and skills that contribute to successful leadership. The present study sought to develop a model that identifies and explains the personal and professional values that influence and contribute to successful military leadership. Many of the models discussed in the literature included the concept and the significance of values to efficient leadership, but none of the literature focused extensively and specifically on identifying and explaining the values that influence and shape the behavior and the practices of successful military leaders.

Another short-coming of existing models in terms of explaining military leadership success is that few models address the need for, and the impact of, such values-based leadership within the context of 21st century world conflict and the GWOT. A unique characteristic of the present study is that the study resulted in citable, contemporary examples that strengthen the theoretical model, and that the model emerged from the data drawn from credible informants who are proven successful leaders.

Summary

Chapter 2 presented a discussion of how the literature review was conducted and a review of the literary sources that address military leadership. The review was accomplished with respect to key and relevant review topics. The topics included a historical overview of leadership; current findings and contributions to 21st century military leadership; leadership styles, characteristics and traits; and a review of the literature concerning the specific context of the study—military leadership and the GWOT.

Literature relevant to the study was located by conducting title searches and reviewing scholarly and peer-reviewed articles, documents, and journals relating to leadership and military leadership (Cone & Foster 2005). Literature providing an enlightened historical overview on the topic of military leadership included studies and biographies of prominent military leaders of both the classical and the modernist era.

With respect to the scope of the literature review, substantial literature was found to be available on leadership styles, characteristics, and traits. More contemporary leadership styles, values, and principles have found their origins in spiritual and religious contexts (Varughese 2008). Servant leadership is one example. The biblical account in which Jesus washed the feet of the disciples (St. John 13:4-5) is an example of leading by serving. Considering the issue of separation of church and state, religion and spirituality, and their relationship to workplace leadership are compelling issues for management practitioners and researchers (Dent et al. 2005). Although some people voice opposition, others support an integrated and objectively definable approach to spirituality in the workplace (Parmley 2005).

Only four significant gaps in the literature were noted. The first and more important gap concerned the lack of literature concerning leadership needs in 21st century unconventional warfare. The specific values that contribute to successful military leadership were also not extensively addressed in the literature. A third gap concerned the lack of a theory-based military ethic focusing on leadership behavior. The final gap was the lack of academically rigorous literature concerning spirituality in leadership in the workplace.

Chapter 2 presented an in-depth analysis of the literature reviewed for the present research study along with a detailed description of the methodology employed. Chapter 3 includes research method and design appropriateness, population, sampling, data collection procedures and rationale, validity, and data analysis.

CHAPTER 3: RESEARCH METHOD

The purpose of this qualitative grounded theory research was to create a model based on the exploration of the values that guide and influence the style and practices of successful military leaders. The study used currently collected data derived from the perspectives and the experiences of eight primary participant subjects who were interviewed. The study also included historical data and data collected from eight secondary participants, those not being studied and not a part of the actual sample size, each having knowledge of one of the primary participants: followers, peers, mentors and others instrumental in the formulation of the values of the primary participants. The results of the study were used to create and describe a model that meets the leadership training goal of developing a force committed to the moral values that represent the foundation and strength of the American military and the American way of life.

The key aspects of the literature review conducted for this research were discussed in chapter 2. In chapter 3, the research method and design appropriateness for the study are provided. The rationale for the use of a qualitative grounded theory research design, including a discussion of why the approach was chosen, as opposed to other designs, are included. The research questions presented in chapter 1 are reviewed and a discussion of the population and sampling, confidentiality and informed consent procedures, geographic location, instrumentation data collection procedures, and data analysis techniques are presented in this chapter.

Research Method and Design Appropriateness

The present study was designed to use a qualitative approach with a grounded theory design. According to Leedy and Ormrod (2008), all qualitative research approaches share two features in common: (a) a focus on phenomenon occurring in natural settings, and (b) the study of such phenomena in their full complexity. Denzin and Lincoln (2005) concurred, noting that phenomenological inquiry, another term used to describe qualitative research, is a naturalistic approach to the world, seeking to understand phenomena in a context-specific and natural setting. The qualitative research approach makes use of its investigative quality in exploring and describing phenomena and examining why certain behaviors are exhibited in terms of the meaning people attach to them (Denzin & Lincoln 2005). Creswell (2007) explained that a major characteristic of qualitative research is the collection of data in the field at the site where the phenomenon is experienced.

According to Mack, Woodsong, MacQueen, Guest, and Namey (2005), as a type of scientific research, qualitative research consists of an investigation that fulfills certain criteria. The criteria include (a) seeks to answer a question, (b) uses a systematic, predefined set of procedures to answer the questions, (c) collects evidence, (d) produces findings not pre-determined, and (e) produces findings that are applicable to situations beyond the boundaries or parameters of the study. The present study fulfilled each of those criteria as discussed below.

Qualitative Approach Appropriateness

The present research study used qualitative methodology to explore, analyze, and interpret the leadership style, behaviors, and practices of successful military leaders as evidenced by the careers of selected senior enlisted military leaders. The phenomenon was studied (a) as it occurred in the natural social setting and (b) in all aspects of its complexity (Leedy & Ormrod 2008). The rationale for research methodology was based upon each of the criteria listed above as suggested by Mack et al. (2005).

Seeks to answer a question. The answer to specific research questions involving how proven military leaders guided, directed, and influenced the actions of followers to accomplish objectives was sought. The specific values that informed and swayed the leadership opinions and practices of the leaders studied were also sought. Other questions this research study focused on concerned the specific actions of the leaders accounting for the success experienced in capturing and sustaining the loyalty, honor, and respect of followers. How the participants met and faced challenges common to all leaders, especially military leaders, was sought.

Uses a predefined set of procedures. The systematic, predefined procedures for answering the research questions involved in-depth interviews and reviews of pertinent historical artifacts and other documentation (Cohen & Crabtree 2008; Creswell 2007; Dick 2005; Hancock 2002). The interviews and document sources were used to collect data on the study participants' history, perspectives, experiences, and values.

Collects evidence. Evidence was collected regarding the success of the style and practices of the leaders from personal testament as well as that of other pertinent participants (Murray 2008). Data from historical artifacts (Cohen & Crabtree 2008; Creswell 2007, Dick 2005; Hancock 2002) and other sources were also used to explore and chronicle the leadership behaviors and attributes of the leaders who contributed to the study.

Produces findings not pre-determined. Although the ultimate success of the leaders is considered a known and well-documented fact, the findings not determined in advance, and those revealed as a result of the study, were the specific values, style, and practices of the leaders resulting in the successful leadership experience.

Produces broadly interpretable findings. The findings were expected to be beneficial when applied to situations outside the immediate boundaries of the study and used to inform contemporary as well as future military leadership situations and circumstances.

In qualitative research, the issue of concern is addressed from the perspective of a specific population related to the research situation (Mack et al. 2005). The present study did so by seeking specific information about the values, opinions, behavior, and practices of several selected military leaders. Understanding the contribution of values to the success of the selected leaders helps solve the problem of how to lead troops successfully in today's military with its unique social and political challenges.

The process in qualitative research is open-ended and involves broad, general questions that facilitate better learning from the participants (Creswell 2007). Qualitative research provides textual descriptions of how people experience the research phenomenon in the purpose statement. A primary benefit of qualitative research methods is the ability to demonstrate social context influence (Shah & Corley 2006). This research relied entirely upon the stated opinions, perspectives, and experiences of the participants within social contexts to develop theory. Qualitative research involves analyzing data such as words, pictures, or objects, whereas quantitative research involves the analysis of numerical data (Neill 2007). Quality refers to the essential character of something; quantity refers to the amount (Cooper & Schindler 2006).

The study findings describe the values the leaders hold that influence their style and practices and make them uniquely successful. Because such an exploratory and descriptive venture is extremely particularistic and difficult to quantify, an unrestricted, heuristic, and qualitative approach was best suited for the study (Menking 2003). No quantifiable findings or data were collected in the study. Context descriptions relied on words and narratives as opposed to numbers, as textual renditions are more effective and advantageous for fulfilling the purpose of this qualitative research objective (Creswell 2007).

Grounded Theory Design Appropriateness

According to Denzin and Lincoln (2005), a qualitative approach combined with a grounded theory research design legitimizes the qualitative approach while providing logic in the specifics of the grounded theory. The grounded theory research design is probably the most recognized technique for conducting qualitative research (Suddaby 2006). Grounded theory methodology produces theory resulting from the systematic gathering and analysis of data throughout the research process

(Strauss & Corbin 1998). In this method, "data collection, analysis and eventual theory stand in close relationship to one another" (Strauss & Corbin 1998, 12). One of the essential elements of the grounded theory research design is that it begins with a preconceived notion or theory in mind. The grounded theory design is appropriate to the present study based on the preconceived notion or theory that the success of the leaders results from certain intrinsically held values because values shape and guide behavior (Bruno & Lay 2006).

The existing literature on values indicated that values and value systems are complex constructs, neither independent, isolatable, nor separate from one another (Levitt, Neimeyer, & Williams 2005; Williams & Levitt 2007). Research also revealed that the military itself, underwent substantial change in adjusting to the nature of contemporary warfare in a fluid global situation (Wong 2003). Under such condition, military forces have found it necessary to assess and train leaders at all echelons to comprehend and adjust to the complexities of making decisions in turbulent times (Carrera & Mastaglio 2006). The grounded theory design is compatible with and adapts well to studies consisting of complex context (Strauss 1987, Strauss & Corbin 1998) such as those mentioned.

The grounded theory approach is appropriate for developing or modifying a theory, explaining a process, and developing general abstractions of people's actions and interactions (Creswell 2007). The culmination of the present research study yielded a theoretical conclusion regarding the specific values that inform and enhance the practice, style, and actions of successful leaders. The study was not intended to test a hypothesis, even though a preconceived notion did exist. The findings were explicitly emergent, and the preliminary goal was "to find what theory accounts for the research situation as it was" (Dick 2005, 4). Glaser and Strauss (1967) suggested that the emergent theory characteristic of the design was the primary feature that differentiated it from other research designs, pointing to the position that "the adequacy of a theory can't be divorced from the process of creating it" (5). The uniqueness of the current study supported a grounded theory approach as the approach helped to build the theory as it emerged from the data collected, rather than from previously existing theories and constructs.

The grounded theory methodology, originating with Glaser and Strauss (Hancock 2002), was mainly identified as the emergence of new theory from the often-simultaneous collection and analysis of phenomenological data, thus exceeding the phenomenology design. Hancock indicated interviews, observation, literature reviews, and documentary analysis are some of the various data collection techniques used to develop grounded theory. In the present grounded theory study, the primary source of data collection involved the interviews of the leaders. Interviews with followers, mentors, and others knowledgeable about the participants enhanced reliability and validity of the study (Murray 2008; Strauss & Corbin 1998).

Design Implementation

Interviewing the sample group in one-on-one dialogues using questions related to the research questions also provided an appreciative and naturalistic inquiry approach to obtaining the required data (Cooperrider & Whitney 2005; Cooperrider Whitney, & Stavros 2005). Appreciative inquiry abandons intervention, focusing on inquiry, imagination, and innovation, using a narrative-based process to move directly to the substance of the information sought. The process is cyclical, according to Cooperrider and Whitney, beginning with engaging the sample group in discussion about strengths, resources, and capabilities.

For the purpose of the present study, the dialog centered on values resulting in characteristics, attributes, and traits causative to effective, and successful leadership. Appreciative inquiry (AI) involves a co-evolutionary search for what is best in people, their organizations, and their world (Cooperrider & Whitney 2005). Appreciative inquiry has largely to do with the art and practice of asking questions that reinforce the capacity of a system to apprehend, anticipate, and enhance positive potential. Essentially, this method of inquiry provides the tools and the clues to make a more powerful difference in the world and in ourselves (Quinn, 2004). This research, as a result of such appreciative and naturalistic efforts and cooperation, yielded results that support the development of values that improve the quality of military leadership.

Research Questions

Successful leaders create a culture that is driven by certain intrinsic values, which become platforms for calls to action and not merely empty platitudes (DiMatteo 2007). The goal of the present qualitative study was to create a model based on the exploration of the values that inform and shape the style and practices of successful military leaders. An underlying assumption was that such a leader earns the right to leadership through legitimacy of power enhanced by concern for the well-being, welfare, training, and readiness of troops, as opposed to self-serving goals and aspirations (Greenleaf 1991; Greenleaf et al. 2002). The research study was designed to reveal the source and type of values and virtues that inform the leadership style and practices of successful military leaders.

The overriding research question (Research Question 1) addressed in the present qualitative study concerned the value system of the leaders: What specific personal and professional values informed and swayed the leadership opinions and practices of the leaders in accomplishing the highly essential and important duties and the responsibilities of their leadership roles? In turn, how do these military leaders successfully guide, direct, and influence the actions of followers to accomplish military objectives effectively?

The research study was constructed to produce specific and citable actions that support and substantiate any claims made. The second question was intended to explore congruency between espoused theory and practiced theory. An objective of this discovery process is to present evidence-based proof by way of personal action citations that account for the success of leaders.

Research Question 2 was designed to reveal and explore specific instances, situations, and circumstances in which the leader in question guided, directed, or influenced the actions of others when focusing on specific goals and objectives. The question asked what specific actions and practices accounted for the success and recognition the leader experienced in capturing loyalty, honor, and respect from followers and peers alike. The aim of this question was also to identify how these actions might be applied to specific leadership scenarios consistent with contemporary challenges faced by military leaders in both garrison and battlefield situations. The second question also considered the personal and professional character attributes and moral views of the leader.

The third research question addressed how successful leaders manage challenges and change, anticipated and unexpected: How do the leaders face and meet the challenges of leadership that all leaders face, from dealing with followers who oppose and resist the process to building up those who need encouragement? Kouzes and Posner (2007) described five challenges that good leaders must confront and be prepared to manage using certain identified methods, and the behavioral commitments they must make to meet those challenges. The purpose of this question was to ascertain how proven successful leaders employ those or similar methods and behavioral commitments to meet such challenges.

The final research question addressed likely existing theoretical leadership models that may be effectively applied to military leadership: What existing theoretical leadership models account for and explain the organizational performance of successful military leaders? The less formal leadership models seem to be gradually replacing the rigid, managerial type models, such as the autocratic style, in recent years (McCrimmon 2007). The present study considered with which models successful military leaders personally identify and to which they ascribe their success.

Population

The population targeted for this qualitative grounded theory study included all senior enlisted military members currently filling or who have previously filled the role of advisor to military installation or military service commanders. A qualitative research approach primarily using in-depth interviews (Seidman 2006) was used in the present study to investigate, analyze, and interpret the leadership values of successful military leaders. Before data can be described or analyzed, it must first be observed (Ayre 2003). Ayre used the term *unit of analysis* to refer to what or who is being observed or explored. Ayre alleged that the unit chosen for analysis must be one that is most relevant to the study. A unit of analysis, sometimes called an element, might be an object, an item, an individual, an event, or groups.

Ayre (2003) advanced that in social science, the individual person is usually the chosen unit of analysis. The unit of analysis is part of a larger population, and the term population is used to describe a complete collection consisting of all the units of analysis, each with one or more characteristics in common that an investigator is interested in studying. The population studied was the composite of all senior enlisted military members fulfilling the role of senior enlisted advisor to U.S. military commanders or to Department of Defense (DoD) organizational commanders. Permission to access the premises and study participants for the primary and secondary participants of both the pilot study and the actual research study were obtained using the documents in Appendix A through D.

Ayre (2003) indicated that both who and what characteristics are studied must be specified. With respect to who was studied, the participants in the present study were senior enlisted members of their respective service. Each participant holds the enlisted rate of E-9, and each fills or has previously filled the role of senior enlisted advisor to the commander of a military command or of his or her DoD organizational commander. The population characteristics studied in this research included leadership style, traits, principles, practices, and habits as they are determined and influenced by personal and professional core values. To answer the research questions, semi-structured interviews with the senior enlisted service members studied and with a secondary group consisting of individuals familiar with the leadership style and practices of the service members were conducted. The research process also included a review of collected artifacts to answer the research questions.

Sampling Frame

Ayre (2003) described a sample as a collection of some of the elements of a population; a subset drawn from the population to represent the population from which it was drawn. Purposive sampling increases the probability of obtaining participants that fit the objectives of the study and the sample criteria (Cooper & Schindler 2006). When investigators intentionally focus on a small number of subjects or cases, sampling procedures are often purposive or theoretical rather than random ("Data Selection" n.d.).

The sampling method used in the present study was purposive since the basis for determining the sample group was selective and limited. The criteria for selecting a sample may be either prior knowledge or suspicion that the sample contains or displays the suspected, desired, or desirable characteristics studied ("Data Selection" n.d.). Purposive sampling procedures fit the goals of the study because the sample group must be proven successful leaders, and consequently must be limited to, and purposefully selected from the population of successful military leaders.

The purposive sampling method is used when an individual subject itself, or a specific group of subjects, is a major focus of the investigation, as opposed to an issue (Teddlie & Yu 2007, 80). In accordance with the concept of purposive sampling, certain participants were identified and selected for this qualitative study, based on the study purpose. The purposive selection of this limited sample emerged as a result of the unique billet held by the leaders, the leaders' successful military leadership careers, and the relationship and acquaintance of the secondary subjects to the leader. Some snowball sampling was also used.

The assertion concerning the success, accomplishments, and qualities of the eight primary participants was based on success at achieving the rank and position held. Third-party testament and well-documented proof of success of the leaders within the military and civilian leadership communities were also sought from secondary, non-study, participants who were familiar with the leaders, including mentors, followers, peers, and other acquaintances. The characteristics of the sample for the study provided confirmation of the leaders' success.

Characteristics of the Sample

The primary participant sample consisted of eight high-ranking enlisted military leaders—two from each of the four major U.S. military branches. Although the study involved 16 interviewees in total (the eight leaders being studied and the eight people who were acquaintances of the leaders), the actual sample size for investigation was eight since only the eight primary participants were actually being studied. Each participant in the sample was considered successful subsequent to achieving appointment to the prestigious and highly visible billet to which assigned. Successful military leaders continually and relentlessly demonstrate certain leadership principles, attributes, and traits (Air Force Doctrine Document 1-1 2006; Department of the Army 2006; Shriberg et al. 2002). Some of the attributes and traits are justice, judgment, decisiveness, initiative, dependability, tact, integrity, enthusiasm, bearing, unselfishness, courage, knowledge, loyalty, and endurance (Air Force Doctrine Document 1-1 2006; Department of the Army 2006; "Marine Corps Leadership Traits" 2007; Shriberg et al. 2002).

The leadership characteristics, traits, and principles discussed here are those typical of successful military leaders of all four military services (Air Force Doctrine Document 1-1 2006; Department of the Army 2006; "Marine Corps Leadership Traits" 2007; Shriberg et al. 2002) including the eight primary participants in the study. Each military service has established similar, if not identical, selection criteria for the equivalent billets. Service members considered for the billet of senior enlisted advisor to organizational and service commanders are thoroughly vetted by a board of high-ranking officers (normally field and general grade officers). The rigorous selection process is exemplified in the precept for the board to select nominees to be considered as the sergeant major of the Marine Corps (SMMC) [Precept] (2003), provided in Appendix E. The precepts typically mandated and applied to the selection process for SMMC are provided as an example of the stringent process used to examine military leaders who are candidates for high-level leadership positions. Those selected are unanimously determined to be the best qualified of all eligible candidates — organization or service-wide.

As participants in the study, the participants must be those identified with many of the qualities associated with exemplary and perhaps transformational leadership. According to Bass (1990), transformational leaders are effective in influencing others because they are charismatic and provide inspirational motivation, intellectual stimulation, and individualized consideration. The participants were those who were reasonably expected to have displayed such characteristics.

The participants' personal and professional accomplishments, military bearing, neatness of appearance, and esprit de corps should be such that they inspire and motivate young troops and other followers to achieve at the highest level of their ability. As the highest-ranking enlisted member of his or her military service or organization, the participants are in a position such that they can persuade continually and encourage younger members to pursue higher education goals and aspirations and to improve and develop their intellectual capacity. Most notable would be the participants' ability to provide individualized consideration for followers, demonstrating and affirming the importance and value of each person.

Sample Size Appropriateness for Data Saturation

Because face-to-face interviewing is preferable due to body language observational advantages (Cooper & Schindler 2006), the sample was composed primarily of military leaders assigned to the five military commands in the immediate geographic area in which the research took place. Only one primary participant was located outside of the immediate geographic area of the research. The relatively small sample size was considered appropriate to achieve data saturation based on the wide range of military leaders represented and consistent with qualitative research characteristics (Cooper & Schindler 2006).

The participant leaders were selected from all four military services — two from each branch. The leaders consequently represented those with a variety of different military and leadership experiences based on the individual service focus and mission. Training requirements and intensity, military occupational emphasis, and service mandates were necessary factors to be considered in the requirement for data saturation. There were two female participants and six male participants among the secondary participants.

Secondary Participants

Secondary participants were extremely helpful and beneficial to this research effort. Secondary participants were those individuals who participated in functions or capacities other than as the central focus of the study. The methodology and procedures included conducting in-depth interviews (Seidman 2006) with the three categories of individuals capable of providing such unique perspectives on the leader. These included leaders and mentors, followers, peers, and acquaintances. The sample size for the secondary participants was ultimately dependent upon identification and accessibility. One secondary participant was selected from among the identified categories of individuals (eight in total) and paired with the corresponding primary participant for a total of 16 interviewees.

Because leadership and leading are indispensable to one another, individuals who have led and mentored these leaders helped provide a perspective on the leaders as followers, and followers were able to reveal the direct effect of the leader's leadership values, character, skills, and effectiveness as a leader. Peers interviewed helped reveal the presence and significance of mutual respect and teamwork that characterize positive peer relationships in the professional life and career of the primary participants. With this in mind, secondary participants representing these categories were involved in the interview process.

Using snowball sampling, the primary participants were asked to identify individuals who have personal and firsthand knowledge of his or her personal and professional leadership qualities and experiences. As noted earlier, these included the participant's leaders and mentors, followers, and peers. A list was made of all potential secondary participants. Participants were selected based upon recommendations of the leaders, agreeability, availability, probability of a good interviewing relationship, accessibility, and other relevant factors (Seidman 2006).

The methodology included the use of historical and documentary information and sources to explore the unique impact of military lifestyle, values, and influences on the leader. For example, Marines live by the values, ethics, and traditions that define the Marine Corps (U.S. Marine Corps 2008). As Marines and citizens, these warriors uphold the core values of honor, courage, and commitment in every situation they encounter. These values shape and mold all military personnel into the warriors they are and highly influence their leadership style and the choices they embrace both as warriors and as citizens.

Informed Consent

According to Eyler and Jeste (2006) and G. E. Mills (2007), the primary goal of the informed consent process is to ensure and preserve the research participants' autonomy by providing complete information regarding the research process, the voluntary nature of the consent, and the assurance that the participants are capable of making such decisions. Participation in this study was voluntary. The standard two-part informed consent process was used (Seidman 2006). The participants were asked to sign informed consent forms and were provided information regarding the extent of their participation in the study. All participants were informed that they could withdraw from the study at any time without any form of reprisal by stating their intent orally or in writing to the researcher.

All study participants (primary and secondary) were contacted by telephone to request their participation in the study. As noted earlier, snowball sampling was used with the primary participants in order to identify secondary participants for the study. Each participant was asked to provide documented informed consent to participating in interview sessions, approximately 90 minutes in length for the primary participants, and 60 minutes for the secondary participants. Appendix F contains the informed consent for primary participants 18 years and older, and Appendix G contains the informed consent for secondary participants, 18 years and older. For participants interviewed in their official military capacity, organizational approval to use premises, name, or subjects was obtained. Appendixes A through D, which have been signed by the appropriate officer of the military command, contain the permission to use premises, name, or subjects. Individual study participants also provided signed informed consent forms.

A copy of the Informed Consent Form (see Appendix F and G) was e-mailed to the participants for execution. All the aspects and the requirements of the study and the informed consent were orally reviewed prior to execution by the participants. The participants were asked to sign the form at the time of the first in-person interview, or prior to the first telephone interview, before beginning the interview questions. The informed consent procedure confirmed that the participants understood and accepted the invitation to be involved in the present study.

Confidentiality

The ethics related to individual research studies should be understood and carefully considered (G. Mills 2007). Steps were taken to ensure ethical procedures and maintain participant confidentiality and anonymity of the source of any information (Creswell 2007). Because the present study involved military personnel, sensitivity of information was also of crucial concern (Murray 2008). Research records and all other data, including contact information sheets, executed informed consent forms, and electronically recorded information, will be maintained in a locked safe or a home office for 3 years, after which all data will be shredded and discarded.

Confidentiality and anonymity were provided for, ensured, and maintained throughout and subsequent to the present research study. Assuring the participants of such measures helped to encourage candor in responses and in sharing of information regarding their experiences, thoughts, and feelings on the topics discussed. Steps were taken from the beginning of the process to code the participant's identity in order to preclude disclosure or divulgence of participant identity information (Seidman 2006). For instance, participants were referred to in the present study by their position or relationship to the primary participants or by an identifier code, as opposed to using personal names or pseudonyms. Third party access to the research data was not allowed.

Geographic Location

All except one of the primary participants were based in the northwest region of the United States. The participants were identified by contacting local commands and requesting referrals of retired and active duty military leaders to participate in the present study. The remaining potential primary participant is located in the Northeast region of the United States. The latter participant is the author of a publication cited in the literature review and a former Sergeant Major of the U.S. Marine Corps who was contacted by telephone. In order to preserve the confidentiality of the participants, only the general geographic locations of the participants have been divulged. The primary participants included senior noncommissioned officers of the four military branches. All secondary participants were located in the same geographical region as the primary participants with the exception of one who was located in the Midwestern United States.

Instrumentation

A wide range of data collection instruments is available for use in contemporary research (Cooper & Schindler 2006). With the increased use of enabling technology, the uses of facsimile, e-mail, the Internet, and Web cameras are increasingly popular means of data collection (Creswell 2007). Cooper and Schindler found interviews can be conducted and electronic questionnaires can be generated and administered by such means.

Selection Appropriateness

Face-to-face, in-depth interviews were the major source of data collection for this research (Seidman 2006). The data collection instruments included an interview guide consisting of open-ended questions developed by the interviewer to guide the discussion (Champion 2006; Creswell 2007; Seidman 2006). Telephonic sources were used as the media source for interviews whenever face-to-face interviews were not possible. Seidman (2006) observed data recording instruments and the interviewer are also instruments to be used in the data collection process.

A major difference between qualitative and quantitative approaches is the recognition and the affirmation of the human interviewer as the data collection instrument (Seidman 2006). Such practice is sometimes condemned based on the effect the instrument may have on the data-gathering process. Seidman argued that the human interviewer should be perceived as an intelligent, adaptable, and flexible instrument with the capability to respond in personal and humanistic ways that non-human instruments cannot.

In addition to the interviewer and the interviewee, a digital voice-recording device was used to capture the words, emotions, experiences, beliefs, and opinions of the interviewees in their own words with accuracy and preciseness (Seidman 2006). An interview guide, as opposed to an interview schedule or open-ended questionnaire (Champion 2006), was used to provide the interviewer with preset questions for which answers were desired (Creswell 2007; Seidman 2006). Seidman cautioned that the in-depth interview methodology is not designed to test hypotheses or to corroborate opinions. The goal of the interview method is to have the interviewees reconstruct their life experiences in an open and uninhibited manner in order to explore their meaning. Any questions should arise typically and ideally from the participant's sharing of information.

A customized interview guide (sometimes referred to in the study as the interview protocol) developed for use as a research instrument in the study was selected over the use of a pre-existing interview protocol or interview schedule (Champion 2006; Creswell 2007). The customized interview guide was chosen due to the potential for flexibility and the ability to customize and construct questions that more closely pertain to the research questions (Creswell 2007; Seidman 2006). Questions can be crafted using this method in such a manner as to ensure that the participant has optimum opportunity to tell the story in his or her own words. Accurate and efficient paper trails were established by using transcription measures to ensure proper records of each interview session (Seidman 2006). These measures included the use of a human transcriber as a research assistant.

Instrument Reliability

The human interviewer should not be decried as a viable instrument in the data collection process (Murray 2008; Seidman 2006). An important consideration is that the interview, through the skill of the interviewer, brings forth and reveals not the interviewer's meaning, but that of the interviewee. Seidman believed the interviewer can be relied upon as the major instrument in the data collection procedure. In the interview method, the dilemma that most other methods present with regard to reliability is confronted. No real guarantee ever exists that research participants are being open, candid, and honest. Even if the information provided by the participants could be determined as trustworthy, the conclusions that follow may not necessarily be transferable to the general population. In other words, "whose meaning is it?" (Seidman 2006, 23).

Because the instrument used to guide the interview process was not a previously validated instrument, pilot testing to reveal any errors in the instrument or the design of the pre-set open-ended interview questions was conducted prior to the research study (Cooper & Schindler 2006). Pilot testing served to refine and ensure the validity and reliability of the questions, as suggested by Sampson (2004) and Yin (2003). Pilot testing was also considered as a means of assessing degrees of bias.

The same procedure described for the actual study was used for the pilot study to include the criteria for the selection of the participants, the leadership category, and the background and characteristics of the participants. The number of the participants was limited to three, all of whom were asked to sign an informed consent letter. Access to and initial contact with pilot study participants was established in the same manner as for the actual research study. Participant selection recommendations were solicited from senior leaders. Based on the recommendations, three participants were invited to participate in the pilot study. The interviews were patterned after the study protocol with identical questions. See Appendix H for detailed piloting/pretesting procedures.

Data Collection

In an attempt to answer the research questions, the grounded theory research design with a triangulation of methods was used in the collection of data to improve reliability and validity (Creswell 2007). In this section, the data collection sources, types, techniques, rationale, and procedures used are presented. The discussion topics included (a) the sources and types of data collected and rationale, (b) data collection techniques and rationale, (c) and data collection procedures.

Types of Data

Data in the form of text using protocol forms or interview guides and recording devices were collected (Creswell 2007). The textual data collected for the study included information on personal and professional background experiences, professed values and value sources, leadership styles, practices, and philosophical views. Information on personal and professional history and leadership experiences to include accomplishments, achievements, and military awards and decorations were useful. These data types were appropriate for the objectives of the study, as they provided evidence of the exceptional leadership style and practices of the subject and the effect of the style and practices on followers and other participants. Any data resulting from interviews with other study participants (those other than the leader/participants) were also helpful in substantiating and corroborating any information generated from the interviews with the leaders themselves (Murray 2008). The data types were appropriate to the qualitative grounded theory design. Locke (2001) asserted that the organizational leadership and management field deals extensively with behavioral issues that are evident in and that arise from the hierarchical structure of the organization.

Data Collection Techniques and Rationale

Impersonal data collection measures such as self-completion question-naires present certain advantages over face-to-face or in-person inter-views (Testa & Coleman 2006). The favorability of questionnaires is due to a greater likelihood of reducing biases and reducing guarded and less than candid responses on the part of participants when using im-personal measures (Champion 2006). Personal interviews afford other valuable advantages. The opportunity to observe facial expressions and body language can be helpful in analyzing participant responses (Seid-man 2006).

While time-consuming, interviewing facilitates the ability to gather valuable data and access the social context of behavior, relationships, and settings, providing understanding and meaning for the behavior (Champion 2006; Seidman 2006). Speaking directly to the leaders in one-on-one interviews is the most direct means of obtaining the infor-mation that answers the research questions (Murray 2008) and of telling the participant's story (Seidman 2006). Because interviews can exceed the limited boundaries of questionnaires and facilitate verbal elabora-tion, according to Champion, the selection of interviews was based on the research goal of seeking insightful information about the values that elicit the characteristics and traits of successful leaders.

If a contact visit in person was not feasible or if the interview could not be in person for any reason, the initial contact established a mutu-ally agreeable time for an in-depth telephone conference to discuss the study (Seidman 2006). Telephonic interviews eliminate the opportuni-ties to benefit from observations and other advantages of in-person in-terviews, but they have some advantages. Either way, as prescribed by Seidman (2006), the purpose of the initial contact visit was fourfold. The contact visit (a) laid the groundwork for mutual respect during the interview process, (b) provided an opportunity to present broadly the nature and context of the study and participant expectations, (c) allowed the interviewer and participant to become familiar with the interview setting when conducted in person, and (d) initiated the process of in-formed consent.

Telephone and Web camera technology afford the capability to administer interviews using other than physical, face-to-face sessions. Depending on the destination of the call and the number of calls to be made, telephone interviews can potentially involve considerable expense (Creswell 2007) but are generally inexpensive and provide some degree of anonymity (Champion 2006; Cooper & Schindler 2006). Web cameras may eliminate this problem to a degree. With either technology, the possibility always exists for interferences caused by technical difficulties. Champion (2006) reasoned the major overriding argument for the use of face-to-face interviewing is the opportunity to observe facial expressions and other body language to ascertain the candor or potential deception of the participants.

Data Collection Procedures

Preparation for data collection is an important consideration. Participants must first be accessed and then contacted (Seidman 2006). The procedures used to access participants for research studies is an important consideration since how access is gained, and how the first contact is made can potentially affect not only the initial relationship but the entire interview process (Seidman 2006). Access for some studies must be gained through what Seidman refers to as "formal gatekeepers" or "informal gatekeepers" (43-45).

For the present study, active duty military participants were accessed through the military command by obtaining permission using the form in Appendix A through D: Permission to use Premises, Name, and/or Subjects. Potential participants were solicited from eight to 10 military installations or other military entities and military retirees in an attempt to obtain eight primary participants. Two primary participants from each of the four military services were selected. Contact was personally made by placing phone calls or sending e-mails to the potential participants to request participation and schedule interviews. Potential non-active duty primary participants were accessed and contacted to request participation personally by making phone calls or by sending e-mails.

The primary source of data collected for the present study involved in-person or telephonic interviews scheduled at a mutually convenient time and place, recorded and carefully and accurately transcribed (Seidman 2006). A limited amount of data emerged from written documents and other historical and biographical data (Hancock 2002). The interview data collection procedures followed in this research was a modified version of those prescribed by Seidman (2006). The main difference is that only one or two interviews were used, rather than three interviews, because similar studies have indicated that participants are often concerned and parsimonious about the amount of time they would be required to spend on the project (Knapp 2009). Because the present study involved prominent military personnel, there was also likelihood that situations such as priority military operations or permanent change of station orders may preclude an extensive amount of time spent on the research.

Each interview session in Seidman's (2006) model was designed for a particular purpose and for gathering information related to specific life and professional experiences of the interviewee as well as for understanding the meaning of those experiences. For this reason, reducing the number of interview sessions required modification of the Seidman model to cover all the interview material (Knapp 2009). In prior research using the Seidman model, Knapp reported that conducting one extensive interview was easier and more efficient. One extensive interview precluded the requirement to spend time at the beginning of each session recapping information previously discussed.

The informational structure and sequence of the established interview procedures were followed as closely as possible, as the procedural structure was intended to serve a specific purpose in itself (Seidman 2006). Each session in a two-session design was approximately 90 minutes in length. If only one long interview was conducted, the session did not exceed 2 hours in length, as suggested by Knapp (2009). Multiple interviews were spaced no longer than one week apart to allow the participant time to think over and consider the past session, but not enough time to result in a disconnect between the two, as Seidman warned.

Each interview session was digitally tape recorded to maintain the reliability and the accuracy of the participant's words (Seidman 2006). Recording the words of the participant offered the benefit of preserving the original words for future checks on accuracy and meaning. The recorded sessions were carefully transcribed for analysis.

As prescribed by Seidman (2006), the first interview in the series (round 1) was designed to gather information from the participant as a result of focused reflection on his or her life history. The goal of session 1 was to put the experiences of the participant into relevant context by learning as much as possible about his or her personal and professional leadership experiences up to the present time. The aim was to find out what events and circumstances brought the participant to the present leadership values, situation, and philosophy.

The second interview (round 2) as explained by Seidman (2006) was intended to reveal information with respect to the participant's present-lived experiences and, in this case, about those acquaintances instrumental in inspiring and influencing the participant's leadership success. The interviewee was asked to concentrate on reconstructing those details as accurately as possible and was encouraged to share information about any relationships that pertained to and impacted upon the topic of study. Leadership experiences and influences as well as relationships with military and civilian followers, mentors, peers, family, and community members were explored. The participants were also asked to reconstruct a typical day experienced as a military leader.

Participants also had an opportunity to reflect upon and to make some sort of connected meaning from the history and the present experiences (Seidman 2006) during the second interview. The participant was asked to consider the information previously shared and reveal any thoughts regarding ways in which those experiences and personal leadership relationships informed and influenced the participant's leadership style, values, and worldview in general. Any clues that revealed the style of leadership and the source and nature of leadership qualities and characteristics that contributed to the success of the participant's professional leadership experience were noted.

Data Reduction and Analysis Process

Before data can be analyzed, they must first be reduced to a manageable size. Following transcription of the interview data for the study, the data were studied, and reduced. In reducing large amounts of data to a manageable size, Seidman (2006) advocated an inductive rather than deductive approach to data reduction and analysis. Such an approach ensures an open mind and the acceptance of conclusions emerging from the text as opposed to matching preformed theories or hypotheses to the data (Cooper & Schindler 2006; Glasser & Strauss 1967). Patton (2002) argued for the usefulness of a combination of the two, as a combination allows moving from

discovering surfacing themes from the interview content to categorizing them according to a framework that emerges from an ongoing repetitive process. The present study followed an inductive approach to data reduction and analysis to remain fully open to themes emerging from the data (Knapp 2009).

Various approaches to the analysis of data are identifiable and available for qualitative research. For instance, Leedy and Ormrod's (2008) five practical steps involved in analyzing data include (a) organization of the details about the study, (b) categorization, (c) interpretation of single instances, (d) identification of patterns, and (e) synthesis and generalization. The Seidman (2006) data analysis plan involves the five steps of (a) marking the text, (b) formulating and analyzing thematic connections, (c) filing categorized excerpts, (d) synthesizing data and responses, and (e) interpreting and generalizing the data.

Grounded theorists employ set procedures and clearly defined steps to develop theory (Creswell, 2005). There are three dominant, identifiable procedures for analyzing data in grounded theory research designs: the systematic, the emergent, and the constructivist approaches (Creswell 2005). The present study used the systematic step-by-step grounded theory data analysis process described by Creswell (2005). This systematic approach to data analysis was selected because the rigor of the process and the specificity of the clearly defined procedures and details inherent in the process lend more credibility to the study, thus enhancing the value of the study for researchers and leadership practitioners. The steps in the process included (a) open coding, (b) axial coding, (c) selective coding, and (d) generating a visual picture, or model, of the theory that emerges (Creswell 2005).

Step 1: Open Coding

In this step, initial categories of information about the personal and professional values of the participants (the leaders) were formulated. The categories were created by segmenting the information collected from the interviews with the primary and secondary participants, any memos and notes taken during or after the interviews, and historical artifacts researched. Categories and sub-categories were identified from the data and included leadership style, leadership influence, professional leadership experiences, personal leadership experiences, and so forth. Even though the study explores and identifies values, no specific values were included in the categories because the intent was that this information would emerge from the data, whether explicitly or implicitly. The open coding categories and the sources were formulated, using the categories and the sources of the information that support the categories.

Step 2: Axial Coding

In accordance with Creswell's (2005) data analysis process, in this step, one open coding category was selected as central to the phenomenon being explored–values contributing to successful military leadership, and related to the central research question. Other categories were then related to the central category as casual conditions (those influencing the core phenomenon), strategies (actions responding to the core phenomenon), and context (specific conditions impacting the strategies). Finally, other categories included intervening conditions (general contextual conditions impacting the strategies) strategies (resultant actions or interactions from the core phenomenon), and consequences (the result of employing the strategies (Creswell 2005).

Step 3: Selective Coding

The selective coding step involved writing a theory derived from the interrelationship of the categories in the model. This theory, according to Creswell (2005), should provide a conceptual explanation for the process being studied. In the case of the present study, the theory identified and explained the values that influence and guide the practices of successful military leaders. According to Strauss and Corbin (1998), this process integrates and refines the theory. The storyline for the interconnecting categories consisted of written and personal memos, developed throughout the process, containing theoretical ideas sorted through to help refine the theory (Creswell 2005).

Step 4: Generating the Visual Picture or Model

The present research study relied on open coding to analyze the data for basic categories and on axial coding to analyze the data for subcategories and specific types of categories. The categories and the interrelationships among them have been represented in a pictorial model providing a conceptualization of the findings. The model has been formulated to provide insight into the values that guide and influence the practice of exceptional military leaders. The model depicts the basic foundation for the success of military leadership, the values that emerged from the foundation, the alignment of exemplifying actions along with the practices and behaviors associated with the values. Thus, the model also suggests the leadership challenges and methods of resolution, and currently existing models and styles that contain import to the study phenomenon. The established model can help meet leadership training goals and act as a day-to-day leadership reference tool for 21st century military organizational leaders.

Reliability and Validity

Two of the criteria used to evaluate measurement tools are validity and reliability (Cooper & Schindler 2006). The use of the concepts of reliability and validity has been common mainly in quantitative research and has recently been reconsidered for use in qualitative research as well (Golafshani 2004). The concepts are different in qualitative studies than they are in quantitative studies (Creswell 2007; Shank 2006).

Reliability in quantitative research deals with consistency and considers whether the study, when repeated, would yield the same or similar results (Creswell 2007; Leedy & Ormrod 2005). Qualitative methods, in seeking reliability, are more concerned with the issues of bias, trustworthiness, authenticity, credibility, and neutrality as opposed to repeatability (Golafshani 2004; Shank 2006). Even though reliability in both research approaches is concerned with accuracy, Shank indicated the described systems relied upon to ensure accuracy of quantitative research become situation relevant in the conduct of qualitative research, depending upon the type or design of the qualitative study. In the present qualitative grounded theory research using interviews, accuracy was ensured by making sure the coding accurately reflected the collected data and by requesting clarification or follow-up information, when necessary, during or after interviews.

Validity in both approaches deals with the truth of the findings. In quantitative research, validity refers to measurement and describes whether the instrument measures what is intended to be measured and the truthfulness of the results (Golafshani 2004). In qualitative research, validity suggests determining if the findings are accurate from all standpoints and "is seen as an advantage of qualitative research" (Creswell 2005, 195-196). Validity can also be defined qualitatively as the degree of similarity or the "closeness of the relationship" between the people studied and the conclusion about the people studied (Warren & Karner 2005, 215). While some disagreement exists as to the conceptual perceptions of truth, most qualitative sources agree, according to Shank (2006), that the stance of the observer/researcher must be made explicitly clear. While the level of stringency used in practicing qualitative science varies, the most critical concern is that honesty is exercised regarding personal perspectives or biases.

Internal Validity

Internal validity of a research study indicates whether or not, and to what extent, its design and the data yielded allow drawing precise conclusions concerning contributory relationships within the data (Trochim 2006). Kohn (1997, n.p.) described internal validity as "a concern for analysis of single and multiple cases." According to Lincoln and Guba (1985), internal validity has to do with how well or to what extent confounding variables are mitigated—an obvious reference to quantitative as opposed to qualitative studies. This qualitative research was constructed to satisfy the goal of internal validity by presenting conclusions that were supported by and consistent with the data resulting from the interviews and other data collection sources.

In the present study, as in all research studies, concepts such as trustworthiness, credibility, authenticity, lack of bias, and neutrality are important. Consideration of these research qualities not only renders the study more rigorous and thus more dependable for the use of other research studies but also more practical and useful for the consumer of the study. The present study resulted in the development of a values-based leadership model that can be used by military leaders in the leadership and training of troops and future military leaders. The importance of moral education and values to the military underscored the pertinence of qualitative research qualities for the present study.

All of the U.S. military services have instituted a set of core values by which its members are cultivated (Chengming 2007). The values include "loyalty, duty, respect, selfless service, honor, integrity, and personal courage" (U.S. Army); "integrity first, service before self, and excellence in all we do" (U.S. Air Force); and honor, courage, and commitment (U.S. Marines and U.S. Navy) (Chengming 2007, 55). Such an intense focus on core values indicates that the military education and training system is significantly committed to the strengthening of the values and morality of its members and inductees (Chengming 2007).

To satisfy the military values requirement, supporting resources such as the emergent model must be deemed credible and trustworthy at the very least. If the study and consequently the model are not considered trustworthy and credible, leaders seeking to improve their leadership skills and effectiveness will find the model useless. Neutrality or lack of bias supports the credibility of the research and the validity of the model. The supporting features of the present study that contributed to the validity of the emergent model included (a) credible and pertinently experienced informants and (b) the trustworthiness of informants based on holding positions of trust in the military organization. Other features included (c) the selection of informants from across the spectrum of military services, and (d) the corroboration of the primary participants' interview results with that of secondary participants experientially knowledgeable about the leaders.

External Validity

External validity facilitates application of results to a broader theory or population beyond the ones considered in the study, "a concern only for analysis of multiple cases" (Kohn 1997, 6). Lincoln and Guba (1985) explained external validity as the strength of the accuracy with which the study findings generalized the conclusions to the entire population. The primary method used for validation is triangulation, which means that multiple data sources and multiple participants must be introduced into the study (Creswell 2005; Kohn 1997). The present study was framed to use data collected from interviews, records, documents, secondary data, and multiple participants to ensure both internal and external validity.

The concept of validity commonly thought of in quantitative research is often rejected because of the innate assumption that a reality exists external to one's personal perception of it (Trochim 2006). It would seem illogical to be concerned with the reality or falseness of an observation pertaining to an external reality, the principle concern of validity. Qualitative research promotes different evaluative standards, sometimes referred to as *validity evidence* (Reynolds, Livingston, & Wilson 2006) for judging research quality.

Lincoln and Guba (1985) claimed that trustworthiness is crucial to establishing the validity and worth of a study. They put forth four criteria by which to meet this requirement. The criteria are referred to as *alternative* versus traditional criteria (Trochim 2006). Traditional criteria are those commonly used in quantitative studies and include internal validity, external validity, reliability, and objectivity (Lincoln & Guba 1985). Lincoln and Guba proposed the alternative criteria for qualitative work are delineated as credibility (paralleling internal validity); transferability (paralleling external validity); dependability (paralleling reliability); and confirmability (paralleling objectivity).

Several strategies or techniques used to establish credibility, transferability, dependability, and conformability in qualitative studies are (a) prolonged engagement, (b) persistent observation, (c) triangulation, (d) debriefing peers, (e) negative case analysis, (f) referential adequacy, and (g) member-checking (Creswell 2005; Lincoln & Guba 1985). Giving a *thick description*–a detailed account–is a technique for establishing transferability; internal audits establish dependability; and confirmability is established through confirmability audits, audit trails, triangulation, and reflexivity (Cohen & Crabtree 2008). The present study made use mainly of several of these techniques, including triangulation of information sources (i.e., interviewing secondary participants and consulting available written documents) to corroborate data collected from the primary participants (Creswell 2005; Kohn 1997).

Even though a restrictive sampling strategy and a small sample were used, because leadership is about people and events (Prewitt 2004; Yeakey 2002), the likelihood of generalization of the study to a wider military population exists. The emerging model may be transferable and adaptable to other organizational situations. While the purpose of this research was not to focus on populations other than those represented by the sample, the context of the data derived from the study did not necessarily rule out the prospect of applicability of the theoretical model beyond those boundaries.

Other populations to which the present study may apply include military leaders who are not at the highest echelon of enlisted military ranks. These military populations are obviously consistent with the context of the study, and generalization is highly likely. The civilian leadership population operates under different social environments, regardless of the basic leadership context–people and events. As noted by Taylor and Rosenbach (2005, 177), military leadership also has a "special heritage" not shared by the civilian leadership population. The study revealed a recent trend toward a more generic/holistic type of leadership focused on people/humanity as the central area of concern within the organization in contrast with the traditional mission-oriented type military leadership.

Summary

The purpose of the present qualitative grounded theory research was to create a model based on the exploration of the values that guide and influence the style and practices of successful military leaders. Chapter 3 described the research approach and chosen methodology for the present study and outlined the systematic process used for the collection and analysis of data. A qualitative approach was selected due to its capability to explore, describe, and explain phenomenon (Creswell 2005; Hancock 2002; Kohn, R. 2008; Seidman 2006). The qualitative research methodology for the study was designed to develop a grounded theory emerging from the data collection process (Dick 2005; Glaser & Strauss 1967) exploring and identifying the intrinsically held values that contribute to successful military leadership.

The chapter presented a brief review of the research questions that were intended to guide the study. The overriding research question inquired about the value system of the participants: What specific personal and professional values informed and swayed the leadership opinions and actions. Three subsequent research questions inquired about congruency between espoused theory and practiced theory by seeking specific citable actions that support espoused theories, how successful leaders manage challenge and change, and whether or not existing theoretical models are being used by successful military leaders.

The selective sample for the present study included eight successful senior enlisted military leaders. The standard, detailed confidentiality and informed consent procedures were followed in the study with all participants, both primary and secondary, being required to provide informed consent statements, and strict confidentiality being ensured. General, regional geographic location was provided rather than exact location as part of a strategy to preserve confidentiality.

Instrumentation and data collection procedures were also discussed in this chapter. The primary data collection instrument included an interview guide consisting of open-ended questions custom-developed for the present study to guide the discussion (Champion 2006; Creswell 2007; Seidman 2006). The grounded theory research design using a triangulation of methods was used in the collection of data to improve reliability and validity (Creswell 2007). Sources and types of data and data collection techniques and rationale were also discussed.

Finally, data analysis techniques, and a discussion on reliability and validity were provided in this chapter. The present study used a detailed step-by-step procedure for the analysis of data consisting of open coding, axial coding, selective coding, and the development of a story line depicted in a model that describes and explains the phenomenon studied. A discussion of reliability and validity was provided to include an explanation of how the categories of internal and external validity pertain to qualitative research. A presentation and analysis of the data collected and a description of the results of the research project are provided in chapter 4.

CHAPTER 4: PRESENTATION

AND ANALYSIS OF DATA

The purpose of the present qualitative grounded theory research was to create a model based on the exploration of the values that guide and influence the style and practices of successful military leaders. The aim was the creation of a values-based leadership model that could be used for training and development purposes for leaders and troops/subordinates. The model can also be used as a practical leadership guide and reference source in the workplace.

The present research study involved investigation into the leadership experiences of the participants, the professed values influencing and guiding their practices and leadership styles as revealed in the data, and their leadership inspirations. A qualitative grounded theory method was selected over other qualitative methods because the theory evolving from the study would be wholly grounded in the data derived from the participants during the data collection phase of the study. Interviews were conducted because they provided an in-depth understanding of the phenomenon being studied, allowing the participants the opportunity to express ideas about the phenomenon in their own words. The researcher had the opportunity to probe and explore more deeply for unrevealed meaning and explanation. Limited artifacts attesting to or indicative of the values and subsequent practices and styles of the leaders were also used to pull out certain themes consistent with the responses.

Chapter 4 presents the findings and analysis results subsequent to the method presented in chapter 3 and describe the systematic application of the methodology. The logical organization of the chapter and the chapter contents include (a) data demographics; (b) data collection; (c) Analysis results; (d) the data transcription, coding, and marking; (e) findings; and (f) data display methods. The chapter closes with a summary and conclusions.

Following the method outlined in chapter 3, an interview protocol containing 28 questions in two interview rounds/sessions was developed (see Appendix I and J.) The custom interview protocol was tested in accordance with the method outlined in Appendix H (Pretesting the Interview Structure) to reveal any errors in the instrument or the design of the interview structure. Subsequent to the pilot test, only minor changes or adjustments were required in the interview protocol and structure. For instance, some of the questions became redundant when the participants had previously discussed the material in earlier questions. In such instances, to avoid redundancy, the subsequent question was skipped or modified as appropriate during the actual study interviews.

A few of the questions required rephrasing when some participants seemed to derive an incorrect intent of the question. For instance, interview protocol question #17 asked about the concept of leaders earning the right to true leadership. A couple of the participants shared that sometimes leaders are appointed based on advancement in rank without necessarily being deserving of a leadership role. The intent of the question was to determine whether the participant felt followers take into account the actions, practices, and behavior of leaders in considering them true leaders regardless of their appointed position or status.

The question was not intended to assess whether or not the participants felt all leaders actually earn the right from followers to assume their leadership status and roles. In such cases, the questions were not changed in the protocol, but were verbally made at the time of the interview if necessary and based on notes taken during previous interviews. Besides interviews, attempts to answer the research question were made by reviewing any available artifacts. These artifacts included works published by the participants (books, articles, and other publications), reports and articles written about the participants, participant biographies, and organizational memorandums promulgated by the participants.

Data Demographics

The present research study was designed to focus on the leadership style and practices of eight military leaders, two from each of the four main branches of the U.S. Military (the primary participants.) These participants included one female military leader and seven male military leaders. Of these, two leaders were African American, one was Hispanic American, and five were Caucasian. The ages of the leaders ranged from 45 years to 60 years old. Included in the study, as secondary participants, were eight individuals (two female and six male participants) familiar with the selected leaders. These included mentors, subordinates, and peers.

The primary participants were either currently serving active duty military members or retired personnel. All study participants except one primary and two secondary were located in the Northwest region of the United States (see Table 1). The demographics of the participants in the study, while not specifically designed to do so, represented a reasonable cross section of the U.S. military population with respect to race, ethnicity, and gender. The diversity within the population demographics made the study more generalizable to the entire enlisted military leadership population.

Table 1

Demographic Characteristics of Data - Primary Participant Gender

Gender	Male	Female
# of Participants	1	7

Table 2

Demographic Characteristics of Data - Primary Participant Ethnicity

Ethinicity	African American	Caucasian	Hispanic
# of Participants	2	5	1

Table 3

Demographic Characteristics of Data - Primary Participant Military Service Branch

Military Service	Army	Marine Corps	Navy	Air Force
# of Participants	2	2	2	2

Table 4

Demographic Characteristics of Data - Secondary Relationship to Primary

Secondary	Subordinate	Subordinate Leader	Superior/ Mentor	Peer
# of Participants	3	2	1	2

Table 5

Demographic Characteristics of Data - Geographic Locations of Primary Participants

Geographic Locations	Northwest Region, U.S.	Southeast Region, U.S.
# of Participants	1	7

Table 6

Demographic Characteristics of Data - Military Status of Primary Participants

Military Status	Active Duty	Retired
# of Participants	5	3

Data Collection

The present qualitative grounded theory research study identified the values most ascribed to by successful military leaders (determined by level of success.) The final theory emerged directly from the data collected throughout the study using triangulation of data sources and types to strengthen the validity of the study. The primary source of data involved participant interviews concurrent with the opinions of Creswell (2007) and Glaser and Strauss (1967). Artifact and documentary analysis was also used to corroborate the results of the primary collected data.

The second interview was designed to ascertain which leadership inspirations (in terms of leaders, mentors, or other influential individuals) influenced the style and practices of the leaders and any values transferred. On two occasions, only one extensive interview was conducted for the convenience of the participant and to eliminate the time needed to recap any relevant material from a previous interview. Each session was recorded in order both to maintain the accuracy of the participants' words and to verify the transcription and analysis.

Analysis Results

Data analysis began after the first recorded interview session and involved the careful transcription of the recordings and reduction of the textual data to a manageable size. The themes, patterns, and terminology emerged by perusing the data in the detailed manner described earlier. Identification of key words and phrases was accomplished by using manual content analysis procedures to group words, phrases and other text suggesting the leaders' values into the categories. Analysis of three specific themes from the data is discussed below.

As noted earlier, three requirements for quality leadership are crucial for a 21st century military force (Avishag 2006; Kondrasuk, Bailey, & Sheeks 2005; Toner 2006). The first and third are particularly relevant to the present study. First was the requirement for leaders who are committed to the preservation of military ethical conventions. The third requirement called for trained leaders committed to improving and enhancing the nobility, integrity, and dignity of human service (Toner 2006). According to the data, the study participants successfully fulfilled these requirements based on their proclaimed values.

The first crucial requirement for quality leadership - the concept of ethics and integrity (morals, beliefs, principles, and values) - was mentioned or alluded to 314 times by all participants combined during the interviews. The fact that every participant brought up this concept and its importance attests to the significance placed on the concept by successful military leaders. Overwhelmingly the leaders agreed that ethical conventions and leadership integrity are indispensable to successful, quality leadership in a 21st century military. Obviously, the concept also transcends the boundaries of military leadership into the realm of civilian organizational leadership.

The requirement for trained leaders committed to improving and enhancing the nobility, integrity, and dignity of human service (Toner 2006) was also indicated by the respondents' statements. The concept of respect — honor, courtesy, dignity in treatment of others, respect for authority, politeness and a desire to serve as opposed to being served was mentioned by the participants a total of 78 times. The concept of servant leadership was clearly evident in the respondents' statements and passionate exchange on this subject during the interview sessions.

Finally, according to the results of the study, successful military leaders practice, not just proclaim, their leadership values, and demonstrate leadership by example. The concept of setting the example or modeling the way was mentioned in the interviews 74 times expressly or implicitly indicating the importance of leadership by example for successful leaders. The data indicated that successful leadership entails discipline, deliberateness of action, and thoughtful calculation in confronting challenges. Discipline was cited as a value 52 times by all eight of the primary study participants and seven of the non-study/secondary participants when discussing the primary. The discipline category included the ability to patiently exercise intellect before emotions in confronting challenges of any magnitude. Six of the eight primary participants made similar remarks when asked to provide leadership advice on confronting challenges.

Data Transcription, Coding, and Marking,

The data were reduced and condensed as the study began, and continued throughout the data collection phase in order to analyze and continually seek meaning in the participants' words. Preparation for data analysis began after the first recorded interview session, and involved the careful transcription of the recordings and reduction of the textual data to a manageable size. Of the three dominant procedures for analyzing data in grounded theory designs–systematic, emergent, and constructivist (Creswell 2005), the systematic approach was used because of the clearly defined, step-by-step process and the rigor of the procedure, lending more credibility to the study. The overall approach to data analysis used for the present study involved constant comparison, sifting, sorting, categorizing, and coding the data during and after the data collection process. After all the data were collected and transcribed, the process turned primarily to open coding, progressing to axial coding, selective coding, and then to the creation of a picture or model of the theory emerging from the procedure.

Once the interviews were carefully transcribed, the transcriptions were studied to gain an overall perspective of the phenomenon as seen through the eyes of the participants. Following the overview of the data, a careful review of the data was conducted in order to capture and note themes, patterns, and terminology that revealed specific values or similar terms and phrases. These were referred to as *values indicators*.

Open Coding for Themes and Patterns in the Data

In the initial step (open coding), initial categories of information about the values of the participants were formulated, based on the information targeted by the research question, to locate themes in the data. The open coding categories were coded as RQ1, RQ2, RQ3, and RQ4. Information from the interviews, artifacts, and other documents were used to answer the research questions. The open coding categories were then matched with specific interview protocol questions (PQs) (see Table 2 and Appendix L). Each RQ was assigned a color so the information in the text responsive to the research question was identified.

Axial Coding

The open coding category represented by RQ1 was selected as central to the phenomenon being explored–values that drive successful leadership cultures and positive cultural influences. This axial coding category was coded as *RQ1SLC–successful leadership culture*. The other three open coding categories were then related to the central phenomenon (producing axial coding) as (a) casual conditions (i.e. actions practices and behaviors of leaders) coded *RQ2APB*, that were conducive to the effective culture represented in the central phenomenon (values-driven culture), (b) successful strategies for facing and overcoming leadership challenges, coded *RQ3LC*, and (c) existing successful theoretical leadership models and styles, coded *RQ4SLTM*, used by the leaders as reflected contextually and practically in their leadership styles and values. The open coding categories for each research question and the related research question are displayed in Table 1.

Selective Coding

The selective coding process was used to derive, refine, and integrate a theory from the interrelationship among the categories (adapted from the research questions) that comprised the model. The theory provided a conceptual explanation for successful military leadership in terms of the values that guide and influence the practices of such leaders. The values, the central phenomenon, were found grounded in the research data and were supported by other data emerging from each additional research question category. Personal memos developed throughout the process regarding themes, congruency of theory and practice, and noted relationships between and among the data comprising each category, present a storyline. During the selective coding process, the data were prepared and analyzed by (a) transcribing the audio into text, (b) developing a Research Question Answer Guide, (c) developing a color coding scheme, (d) carefully reading through the text, and (e) marking/highlighting the text for themes and patterns using the color code.

Transcribing the audio data to text. The audio recordings of each of the 16 interviews (eight primary and eight secondary) were carefully converted into text. At this stage, all identifying terms and names were removed from the transcripts to avoid disclosing the identity of the participants. Any sections or passages in the audio recordings that could not be clearly discerned were marked in the text as inaudible. Non-standard /military terms, jargon, and phrases were parenthetically explained.

Table 7

Formulating Open Coding Categories

Open Coding Category & Sources [Applicable Protocol Question (PQ)]	Research Questions
RQ1 (Leadership Values) (4, 8, 9, 10, 11, 15, 20, 25, 26)	What specific personal and professional values informed and swayed the leadership opinions and practices of the leaders in accomplishing the highly essential and important duties and responsibilities of their leadership roles?
RQ2 (Actions, Practices, Behaviors) (6, 9, 17, 18, 19, 21, 24, 25)	What specific actions and practices accounted for the success and recognition the leaders experience in capturing loyalty, honor, and respect of followers and peers alike?
RQ3 (Leadership Challenges) (12, 13, 14, 16, 19, 22, 23)	How do the leaders face and meet the challenges that leaders face, from dealing with followers who oppose and resist the process to building up those who need encouragement?
RQ4 (Theoretical Leadership Models) (2, 3, 5, 15, 19, 20, 21, 22, 24, 25, 26)	What theoretical leadership models account for and explain the organizational performance of successful military leaders?

Developing a research question answer guide. A Research Question Answer Guide (see Appendix L) was developed to assist in locating and revealing the answers to the research questions within the text. The first step in developing the answer guide involved annotating the interview protocol instrument. The process involved placing a corresponding number representing the research question (RQ1, RQ2, RQ3, or RQ4) next to the protocol question designed to answer the research question or that may potentially or incidentally provide answers to the question. The annotated interview protocol instrument was then converted to a research question answer guide to provide a systematic procedure for answering the RQs. The answer guide provides locations within the transcript where potential answers may be revealed. The answer guide included the color coding used to mark the text in the subsequent step.

Develop a color code/highlighting scheme. In this step, a color code/scheme was determined to help identify the data in the text relating to or providing the answer to each RQ. Yellow was used for RQ1 and identified in the text any specific values or concepts representing or signifying values (values indicators). Green highlighting (for RQ2) represented text revealing specifically citable or obvious actions, practices, or behaviors and attitudes of the participants congruent with espoused or professed values and behavior from RQ1. Pink highlighting (for RQ3) indicated textual data revealing the participants' response to organizational challenges. Text highlighted in blue (for RQ4) revealed leadership models, theories, or styles expressed by the leaders as their personal leadership identity or those congruent with the actions, practices, and behavior of the leaders.

Any artifact data collected and used were treated in the same manner as the transcribed interview data and integrated with the data collected for the corresponding participant. Artifacts included participant biographies, articles written about the participants, works published, and other documents such as memorandums and papers written by the participants. Artifacts were not available for all participants.

Carefully reading through the text. A careful review of the text for each interview and all artifacts was conducted to gain a more thorough familiarization of the interview data and the participants' leadership values, styles, and practices. The review was intended to find any themes or common threads that may be helpful in determining commonly shared values and the origin of those values. The text was again perused in subsequent steps with a focus on each individual RQ.

Marking/highlighting the text for themes and patterns using the color codes. In this step, the research question answer guide was used to determine which protocol question (PQ) potentially contained answers to the RQs. The transcribed text and artifacts data were searched in a detailed manner for specific answers in the areas of the text indicated in the answer guide, and for incidental answers embedded elsewhere. These occurred in the form of either conceptual or concrete answers to the RQs. The interview and artifacts text were highlighted using the appropriate color. The procedure was repeated for each of the 16 participants for each of the research questions.

Because qualitative research generates massive amounts of data, the data must be reduced to a manageable size and type for display. Data display takes several forms, all with the benefit of condensing the data for ease of interpretation, visualization and understanding, for both the researcher and the consumer. The various alternative forms of data display also provide a more compact and visually stimulating means of sharing the data than do pure narratives. The data for the present study are displayed using charts, graphs, diagrams, tables, and matrixes.

Findings in the Data

The findings for this qualitative grounded theory study were analyzed, based on the major themes or patterns that become evident in the data responding to each research question. The findings were organized and presented, based on the major themes that arose from responses to the research questions. With the exception of the first question, each of the protocol questions was designed to explore and reveal answers to at least one of the four research questions. The broad and overarching research question—Research Question 1 (RQ1) formed the theme and central phenomenon of the study, and was supported by the three subsequent research questions (RQ2– RQ4). Interview Protocol question number one (PQ1) was designed to establish and support the legitimacy and the validity and reliability of both the selective sample and the research tool by providing a framework relative to the leader's experience in terms of type of experience and duration and totality of experience.

Theme 1: RQ1SLC- Successful Leaders Care

The major theme that emerged from the data responding to the first research question was that successful military leaders genuinely care for followers. This concept formed the central value in the leadership model. The specific values mentioned in the care values category include care, compassion, consideration, kindness, people, sympathy, empathy, love, concern, safety, passion, emotion, and diversity. They were expressly mentioned by the participants in terms of looking out for the well-being and the welfare of troops, followers, or subordinates. This response also included any indication of valuing and loving the whole person. Participant P6 stated, "Everything is about people to me because my biggest fault in life is that I love people. And if anybody asks me what I love the most in life, it's people... when you love people, and love them truly and honestly, they'll love you back."

This category also included an appreciation and tolerance for diversities among people in the workforce. These values were made mention of 322 times throughout the entire study by all of the participants combined. Each participant mentioned this value several times; 11 out of 16 participants making mention more than 10 times throughout the interviews.

Sub-Themes. The other prominent leadership values revealed by the study represent sub-themes–those that result from the major theme emerging from the data. The values listed represent sub-themes that occurred or were mentioned frequently throughout the research. The frequency of mention for each sub-theme is shown in parentheses:

1. *Integrity (319)* — honesty/truth, directness, transparency and genuineness, ethical character, virtue, morals, right choices, do the right thing, good judgment.
2. *Service (264)* — Serving others first, selflessness, sacrifice for others, helping and supporting others by mentoring, counseling, giving and contributing, encouraging and motivating, helping and supporting, mentorship and counseling, follow-up and feedback, giving and contributing, encouragement, motivation, and building others up.

3. *Intellect and intellectual stimulation (148)* — growth and development, improvement, wisdom, knowledge, understanding, common sense, education, training, learning, and teaching.

4. *Family values (118)* — concern for family, traditional family oriented values and feeling, early home training, and values.

5. *Knowing and relating to subordinates (114)* — Knowing their needs and interests, understanding/insight into people/ability to relate and interact, relevancy, understanding and insight into people, rapport, remaining current, being in touch and involved, awareness.

6. *Loyalty (103)* — patriotism and dedication to country, loyalty to superiors and subordinates, disagreeing in private, presenting a unified front, patriotism and dedication to country, and commitment.

7. *Trust (98)* — trustworthiness, dependable, responsibility, accountability, punctuality, worthy of confidence and faith, doing your duty/job.

8. *Leadership (87)* — inspiring and influencing, self-leadership, impacting, and making a difference.

9. *Positive attitude (19)* — A good attitude, persistency, a *can do* attitude, never give up, optimism, enthusiasm, good nature, enjoyment, a sense of humor, fun, and personal dynamism.

10. *Respect (78)* — honor, courtesy, dignity in treatment of others, respect for authority, and politeness.

11. *Setting a good example (94)* — model the way, hands-on instruction, and learning.

12. *Appreciation (73)* — Admiration and approval of others and their contributions and abilities, belief and confidence in subordinates and superiors, and recognition.

13. *Work (52)* — Hard work and dedication, commitment, going above and beyond duty, mission accomplishment, and success.

14. *Cooperation and team work (63)* — mediation, unit cohesion, mutual care, input, brotherhood, morale, brotherhood and camaraderie, peace, harmony, togetherness.

15. *Discipline (52)* — self-discipline and self-control, calmness, even keel, intellect over emotions, consistency, endurance, quiet leadership, candor, and tact.
16. *Pride and professionalism (51)* — maturity, military bearing, ability to command attention, command presence, military neatness of appearance and physical fitness, and passion.
17. *Expertise (49)* — excellence, experience, proficiency and knowledge, efficiency, attention to detail, and prioritizing.
18. *Equality (44)* — Fairness/consistency, democracy, affecting the masses, benefits to all.
19. *Communication (43)* — relationships and cultivating relationships

Theme 2: RQ2SLAPB – Successful Leaders Practice their Values
The actions, practices, and behaviors of the leaders reveal the casual workplace conditions that result from and are driven by the central phenomenon (values). The successful leadership style as evidenced by the cultural conditions established in the workplace is caused by the values learned, lived, and professed by the leaders as they lead their organizations. These sub-phenomena validate the influence of the leaders' values on their behavior. RQ2 focused on exploring and revealing those actions, practices, and behaviors (APB).

Sub-Theme: Model the Way. A pattern emerged revealing that a common action among participants was their tendency to set personal examples (often on-the-spot) for followers to emulate. A sampling of participant statements revealing the theme follows:

1. Participant SP7 stated, "He actually came down there, as a Master Chief C.O.B., he actually came down there and cleaned with us for at least an hour…Even though he was our senior, he tried to show the guys that he wasn't above doing what we were doing."
2. Participant P1 stated, "I got down and cleared the weapon."
3. Participant P3 stated, "I made it a point to be the first one there, to be the one that got bloody first, tore up their clothes…

and I might not have stayed out there and strung all the wire with them, but I was out there the first 20 minutes with them." Modeling the way, or setting the example was mentioned 74 times in the data and was the 13th most frequently occurring value out of 200 values mentioned.

Sub-Theme: Knowing and relating to subordinates. One of the most common practices among the participants was that of intentionally becoming familiar with each subordinate on a personal basis, their family members included. This practice reflected the values of family, establishing and cultivating relationships, insight into people, knowing and relating to subordinates, and understanding subordinates' needs and interests. For instance, participant P1 stated, "I knew every one of my platoon sergeants, I knew their spouses' names, I knew their kids' names."

Participant SP7 stated, "He seemed to know everyone's name and any issues that were going on. He always wanted to know what was going on with your personal life... he would go into each work center space and introduce himself."

This practice was described by participant SP7 as "intrusive leadership" in a positive sense. Knowing and relating to subordinates was mentioned 114 times in the data and was the fifth most frequently occurring value.

Theme 3: RQ3LC–Successful Leaders Face Challenges using Intellect over Emotions.
Successful leaders strategize in both facing challenges and challenging the ordinary process of things in their organizations. Leaders do this by searching for opportunities, experimenting, and taking risks (Kouzes & Posner 2002). RQ3 focused on how successful leaders respond to leadership challenges and take beneficial risks to overcome significant challenges in leading their organizations in order to create leadership cultures conducive to work, training, and development.

Research Question 3 revealed themes associated with behaviors exhibited by the participants as they responded to and dealt with various leadership challenges. Based on the themes that emerged, data indicated that the leaders approached challenges with the same calm and deliberateness they customarily employed in their normal day-to-day leadership activities. Participants indicated a calm and calculated response to resolving problems and challenges. Each advised that a thoughtful, deliberate, and well thought-out response yielded the best results and outcomes. The research revealed one very typical example of such a response exemplifying this particular behavior. Participant P6 used the phrase "intellect over emotions" describing it as the "McMichael Rule." The participant used this concept to move past the initial moment of anger caused by the challenge he faced, and respond with rational intellect.

Participant P3 advised, "Sit down, envision the outcome, and then chart your course to the outcome…patience, listening, and then action." A deliberate calculated approach to resolving an organizational challenge by researching the source of the challenge to determine how best to react was also evident. Participant P4 said, "I started reading more books on leadership, trying to read about the generation." The ability to exercise intellect as opposed to emotions requires discipline and self-control. Discipline was mentioned 52 times during the data collection phase and was the 15th most frequently occurring value concept.

Theme 4: RQ4STLM–Use of Existing Successful Theoretical Leadership Models/Styles
The autocratic leadership and management style are typically associated with military leadership. A recent shift has become evident across the military services based on a less formal and more persuasive influence rather than one predicated on position and status (McCrimmon 2007.) RQ4 focuses on identifying those successful theoretical leadership styles and models (STLM) currently used by successful military leaders in context, and the values reflected in those models. The major sub-themes that arose with respect to the fourth research question revealed the characteristics associated with four major leadership styles.

Sub-Theme 1. Servant leadership characteristics were evident when the participants discussed the concept of service as a leadership value.

Twelve out of 16 participants made statements reflecting the servant leadership characteristic of *desire* to serve *first*. For example, the Air Force core value of service before self was frequently mentioned by Air Force participants. The servant leadership characteristic of putting followers before self was mentioned by 13 out of the 16 participants. Other frequently mentioned servant leader characteristics included listening, empathy, awareness, and a strong ethical code.

Sub-Theme 2: Transformational leadership characteristics were evident when participants revealed or discussed such characteristics as follower admiration, respect, and trust. More than 50% of the participants displayed this characteristic. The moral conduct, ethics principles, and values theme were mentioned or indicated by 13 out of the 16 participants.

Sub-Theme 3. Situational leadership characteristics were apparent when participants indicated the use of this style of leadership. Seven out of the eight primary participants advocated and professed the use of situational leadership. A typical statement made by Participant P3 was, "The best style is whatever that person [the follower] needs. I think it's situational more than anything else…You just have to be able to move between them and understand when it is appropriate."

Sub-Theme 4. Participative decision-making leadership characteristics also emerged from the responses of seven out of eight primary participants. Participant P3 clearly stated, "Predominantly, I like to operate in a participative zone when possible, because the other thing I realized when I got older is I am smart enough to know that I'm not all that smart." Participant P1 noted, "I use various contacts throughout the installation… I tend to sit back, gather information, and then make a better more informed decision."

Outliers. Some of the responses may be considered outliers since only a few of the participants made mention of them. Only two important outliers were noted with respect to leadership values mentioned by the leaders. Only 2 of the 16 participants mentioned *consensus building* as a leadership value (each mentioning the value only one time). Participant P1, in discussing the value of team building stated, "I think that what's important to me is team building…it's not always necessary, but absent consensus, I have no problem making a decision. But to get buy-in from the folks, no matter what the situation, and to let them be a part of it and to assume ownership of it, it's been my experience that the output is greater."

Another outlier was the value of *direction* (or providing direction.) Only 3 of the 16 participants mentioned *direction* as a value–one participant mentioned the value two times, and the other mentioned it only once. Even though these responses of consensus-building and direction can be considered outliers, the number is not necessarily indicative of the lack of unanimity or the relative importance of the value of consensus-building among the entire sample – only that the specific discussion did not turn to the concepts in the other interviews.

Displaying the Data

The data for RQ1 (axially coded) were extensive and consisted of every value or value indicator driving leadership actions and made mention of specifically or indicatively during each research interview (excluding the pilot study interviews.) A total of 16 interviews resulted in massive amounts of data to be reduced to a manageable size and type. More than 200 specifically named values emerged from the 16 interviews. These values were eventually, and in an on-going fashion, condensed into 40 *values categories* encompassing the overall concept related to the values in each category.

Some of the more frequently occurring values were *Care, kindness, people compassion, sympathy/empathy, consideration, love, concern, safety, and human dimension*. These were combined into one category labeled caring, etc. The *Leadership Values* graph (Figure 2) depicts the relative value of the 21 most frequently occurring values/values indicators by category. Less frequently occurring values and those not relative to any of the established values categories were considered relevant to the concept of successful leadership, but were not included in the final values graph. The individual values were categorized into 40 more manageable groups of similar and definably the same values and graphed for visual conceptualization. Only the 21 most frequently occurring values are shown on the Leadership Values Graph (Figure 2).

The purpose of this RQ was to provide clarity of understanding for the research consumer as to how the leaders related their values to their practices and to demonstrate congruency between the professed values and the actions, practices, and behavior of the participants (or *praxis*—espoused theory and theory in practice). The data were again perused with the aim of noting any mention of specific and citable actions, practices, and behaviors of the leaders that reveal congruency with the professed values.

The most suitable manner for display of the data emerging from RQ2 was a matrix because no relative or comparative values or frequencies of occurrence apply—only informational and explanatory concepts were of interest. RQ2 represented only *specific* and *citable* evidence of the congruency between the participants' espoused theory and their practical theory (what they actually did), their (*habitual*) practices, and their behavior and attitudes. The recorded results were triangulated by the use of the data from not only the primary participants, but also data from secondary participants, and various artifacts researched.

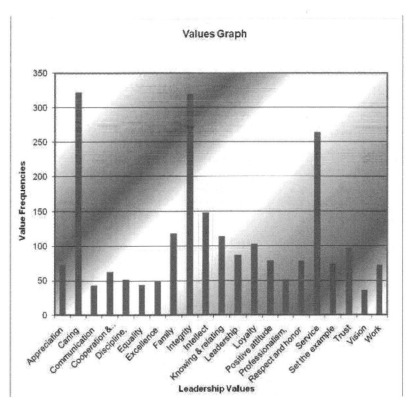

Figure 2. Leadership values frequency graph.

The purpose of RQ3 was to determine how the leaders met and responded to organizational and personal challenges. The RQ3 data were organized in table format, displaying the participants, their most memorable leadership challenge, their responses to the challenge, and their advice to leaders facing their own leadership challenges. The visual comparison revealing any trends, relationships, or similarities between the participants' experiences, responses to the challenges, and advice provided by the participants facilitated the analysis.

Matrixes were used to reduce and display the data for RQ4 consisting of existing theoretical leadership models and styles. RQ4 concerned existing theoretical leadership models and the organizational performance of successful military leaders. The responses to protocol questions #2 and 3 were used to identify the existing leadership theories, models, and styles with which the participants identified. The interview transcripts were once again carefully examined in detail focusing on any contextual mention or indication of existing leadership styles, theories, or models.

Summary

A major thematic pattern noted in the data findings was the frequency of the value the participants described as caring for followers and other values that naturally follow as a result of expressing or showing care. The value described as care included concepts such as love, compassion, concern, and consideration. This theme revealed information useful in answering RQ1.

Other major themes found in the data were related to the other three research questions. The actions, practices, and behavior of the leaders (RQ2) presented major common themes found in the participants' responses and statements. The most common practice among participants was their tendency to set personal examples for followers to emulate. A third important theme in the data revealed how the leaders faced and overcame leadership challenges (RQ3). Themes in the data indicate that the leaders approached challenges with calmness and deliberation. Participants, by their express statements, advocated and advised a calm and calculated response to resolving problems and challenges. Each advised that a thoughtful, deliberate, and well thought-out response yielded the best results and outcomes. Finally, the data findings reveal that servant leadership, transformational leadership, participative decision making, and situational leadership are existing theoretical models and styles that are practiced by successful leaders.

Chapter 4 presented the findings from the data gathered during the data collection phase of the research. Chapter 4 also provided relevant quotations of the participants that helped clarify and support the findings in the data and illustrate the themes. Chapter 5 presents the findings relevant to each research question, the study implications, recommendations, and suggestions for further research.

CHAPTER 5: CONCLUSIONS

AND RECOMMENDATIONS

Chapter 5 includes a discussion of the study findings that were presented in chapter 4 of this qualitative grounded theory research study on the values that influence and guide the style and practices of successful military leaders. Chapter 5 is organized according to the four themes in chapter 4 responding to the research questions. The answers to the research questions supplied the defining elements of the leadership model resulting from the study and also presented in the conclusions. Besides a discussion of the research question findings derived from study, this chapter also presents study implications of the resulting themes as they compare and contrast with the Chapter 2 literature review findings. Recommendations and suggestions for further research are also presented.

The specific problem addressed in the study was the lack of credible qualified leaders to respond adequately to the training and leadership demands of a 21st century military (Defense and the National Interest 2007). Although many personal attributes and qualities interact to determine the effectiveness of those in leadership roles, perhaps the most crucial underlying determinant of behavior and effectiveness is that of values (Bruno & Lay 2006). A model depicting the values that contribute to leadership success will benefit consumers who are researchers in the field of military leadership as well as military leadership practitioners. Researchers may build upon and improve the theory from which the model was derived (including the model itself), and military leaders can apply the model to their own day-to-day practices as troop leaders. The resulting model not only contains a detailed delineation of the specific values that were ascribed to by proven successful military leaders, but also the types of actions practices and behaviors they consequently portrayed. The model also demonstrates advice for overcoming leadership challenges of any type or magnitude and the existing leadership styles and models that also contribute to success. Organizational leaders aspiring to success as leaders in any venue may find the results of the present study beneficial conceptually, theoretically, and practically.

The goal of the study, using a qualitative grounded theory approach, was to determine what specific values account for the success of successful military leaders. This concept was the focus of the main research question (RQ1) and represented the central phenomenon of the study–determining the leadership values that influence and guide the style and practices of successful leaders. The study was also focused on determining (based on RQ2) what specific actions, practices, and attitudes accounted for the success the leaders experienced in capturing loyalty, honor, and respect from followers and peers alike. Responses to this question also helped to verify the values claims by citing specific actions, practices, and behaviors congruent with the claims of the leaders. RQ3 and RQ4 respectively explored the leaders' approach to overcoming challenges, and the leadership styles, models, and theories contributing to the success of the leaders.

Data Findings

The conclusions of the study, with respect to the findings pertinent to each RQ, present a concrete conceptualization of the resolution of the problem addressed by the study. The entire focus of the study was upon answering the research questions with the intent to determine what values account for the effectiveness of successful of military leadership. With this focus in mind, this section will discuss the study conclusions for each research question based on the themes that emerged and will compare and contrast those themes with the chapter 2 literature review.

Theme 1: RQ1—Successful Leaders Embrace the Value of Care
What specific personal and professional values inform and sway the leadership
opinions and practices of successful military leaders in accomplishing the highly
essential and important duties and the responsibilities of the leadership roles
they hold as senior enlisted advisors to organizational commanders?

The themes in the data suggested that the style and practices of successful military leaders are guided and influenced by a wide range of ethically and morally based values and practical mission oriented values. More specifically, the data indicated that the participants, representing the wider enlisted military leadership population, were guided by more than 200 different individual values. The most frequently occurring themes were those suggesting values found in the *Care* category. These types of emotional values represented the human dimension of leadership and arose from the overall emotion of love for people, forming the basis and the foundation of the leadership model resulting from the present study. By definition, love is "unselfish loyal and benevolent concern for the good of another: as (1): the fatherly concern of God for humankind and (2): brotherly concern for others" (Merriam-Webster Online Dictionary 2010). The premise then is that a love of people is at the heart of successful leadership, regardless of the venue. Further speculation (based on the love concept) is that successful leadership is pure leadership– it does not change when applied to various different venues.

The values comprising the care values category (those that stem from the human love concept) include care compassion, consideration, kindness, people, sympathy, empathy, love, concern, safety, passion, emotion, and diversity. Not only are the humanistic/care and emotional values outgrowths of the human love concept, but from the care values arise all the other prominent leadership values. Additional themes suggested other prominent leadership values that emerged from the data and were discussed in chapter 4. No prior research was found with specific references to values that influence and guide successful military leadership.

Theme 2: RQ2SLAPB –Successful Leaders Practice their Values
What specific actions, practices, and behaviors account for the success and recognition the leaders experience in capturing the loyalty, honor, and respect from superiors, followers, and peers alike?

The study revealed many actions, practices, and behaviors that impact the success and the reputation of the leaders and that reflect the values professed by the leaders. Ample data responding to this research question were collected. Themes in the data also highly supported the participants' claims concerning their guiding and influencing values, the overwhelming majority of which stemmed from a caring and humanistic approach to leadership.

A common theme in the data concerned the practice among participants to set personal examples for followers to emulate. These actions also showed followers that the leader cared enough to come down to their level in order to be effective and that they were not above participation in team work. According to participants, such actions were instrumental in capturing the loyalty, respect, and willing obedience of subordinates.

Theme 3: RQ3LC–Successful Leaders Face Challenges using Intellect over Emotions.
How did the leaders face and meet the challenges of leadership that all leaders face, from dealing with followers who oppose and resist leadership actions and processes to building up those who need encouragement?

The behaviors exhibited by the participants also provide an indication of how successful military leaders responded to and dealt with various leadership challenges. Such leaders approached their leadership challenges with the same calm they customarily employed in their normal day-to-day leadership activities. This phenomenon not only reflected the value of calmness, but also that of consistency, discipline, self-control, an even-keel demeanor, and responding with intellect rather than emotions.

Theme Four: RQ4STLM –Use of Existing Successful Theoretical Leadership Models/Styles.
What existing theoretical leadership models account for and explain the organizational performance of successful military leaders?

The final research question was focused on the effectiveness of existing theoretical leadership models and styles. Protocol question #2 elicited data and information from the participants as to which styles and aspects of existing models they felt served them well and contributed to their success as military leaders. The participant's explicit claims as to professed leadership styles were noted and recorded in the data display. Other data also provided obvious indications regarding the participants' use of and adherence to existing styles.

The themes emerging from RQ4 revealed that many, if not all successful military leaders possess tendencies toward both servant leadership and transformational leadership. Even though the participants did not expressly state that they used these leadership styles, data indicated that they often operated in servant and transformational leadership roles, based on the servant leadership and transformational leadership characteristics (Barbuto & Wheeler 2007; Bass, Avolio, Jung, & Berson 2003; Greenleaf 1997) they exhibited.

Themes from the data presented in chapter 4 indicated that the use of situational leadership was prominent among successful military leaders. Prior research by Yeakey (2002) corroborated this finding, noting the importance of adaptive leadership in today's military environment with its complexities and ambiguities. Most of the participative decision-making styles used by successful military leaders fall into the consultation, joint decision making, and delegative styles indicating the leader's perspective on the sharing of power as Yukl (2010) concurs. Autocratic decision-making procedures are typically reserved for extreme or rare circumstances such as combat situations or a need for urgent decisions. Successful military leaders use the autocratic decision-making style increasingly less as they grow and mature in their leadership careers.

Study Implications

There is a general (though not unanimous) consensus among the study participants that recent methods to improve and enhance both the training of the troops and leadership development have been met with success. Such indications reveal the success of the leadership styles employed by the leaders. According to the study, values comprise the fertile ground for the cultivation of successful leadership environments and cultures that stress morals and ethical behavior in organizational leadership and management. A values-based holistic and humanistic approach to leadership necessarily means that the leader sees and approaches leadership from a holistic and humanistic perspective. This perspective reflects upon the values of the leader as revealed in personal actions, practices, and behaviors, and is also exemplified in the predominance of the leader's intellect over emotions (the McMichael Rule.)

The Holistic Approach and Concept

The results of the study supported the position that successful military leaders evolve and adopt their values-based approach over the years due to professional leadership experience. Successful leaders also overwhelmingly seem to have solid foundations of leadership stemming from total life experiences and family values (those taught in the home from an early age). The holistic aspect of leadership points to and supports the flexibility of the style as a whole-life approach effective in all leadership venues including family, corporate, academia, political, religious, and military areas.

The holistic concept means that leadership itself at its best is a total life experience, taking into consideration the total life of the follower as well. One participant noted that a military leader can never accept isolation to a purely military mindset coming from a society environment to which they (and followers) must eventually return. The participant went on to explain that it is an insult to one's intelligence to allow one to be one dimensional while attempting to live and survive in a holistic world. Absent such a holistic and life-encompassing approach, transitioning from a military sub-society into mainstream society would be problematic because the individual would have become accustomed to the military lifestyle. Leadership from this perspective reflects upon the leader's humanistic values as well as reflects a concern for the whole person.

Also implied in the holistic approach to leadership is the notion that rather than focusing on the transferability of military leadership to the civilian sector, one realizes only one variety of true leadership exists. As one participant expressed, "leadership is leadership." Particular leadership venues (i.e. military or civilian) are not to be considered adaptable to one another; instead, the leadership phenomenon may be adapted to serve the particular needs of the various leadership venues.

The Humanistic Approach and Concept

A humanistic approach to leadership genuinely recognizes and values foremost the people of the organization and their unique gifts and contributions. This approach is important because, as the study revealed, leaders adopting this approach view people as the heart of the organization providing the impetus that drives the organization toward its goals and mission. The "mission first, people always" mantra was a connecting thread or theme throughout the study. The mission is important, but without the feeling of community and care (taking into consideration the individuals and those who support them—their families), the mission cannot be as effectively accomplished, if at all. Placing service members and their support network first enables the members to focus on the mission in the performance of their duties.

The McMichael Rule–Intellect over Emotions

Participant P6 discussed the significance of leaders being governed by intellect rather than emotions–the McMichael rule (McMichael 2008) when faced with challenges. Any type or magnitude of challenge may be effectively met and overcome by controlling initial emotions, rising above the situation, and gathering the necessary information to make a rational and successful decision or response. Irritation, anger, frustration, excitement, rage, and anxiety are examples of emotions that cloud judgment and diminish the capacity to think and act rationally and intelligently. The participant shared the following experience when facing a particular personal challenge.

The one paper that tells the Marines' story labeled me as a "poor choice," and they didn't even know me. They didn't even interview me. They didn't even take the time to research my credentials, but I was a "poor choice." And that was a challenge I could have taken negatively and said, "I'm going to spend the next four years in misery because rather than help, everybody is going to be trying to pull the rug from under my feet…you have to take all that and push it aside and keep a positive attitude. And how I combated that: I simply took the article from the Marine Times that said I was a poor choice, and got past the moment of anger or emotion, and practiced the McMichael rule. I got intelligent and took it to Kinko's and had it framed and matted and hung it in my office over my desk. So every day that I came in, there was a reminder of reaching for excellence."

The intellect-over-emotions concept helps leaders face and resolve many types of challenges. Conversely, Participant P7 pointed out the value of showing these types of emotions, as opposed to stoic resignation and passionless response, because they make leaders appear approachable, amenable, and relatable.

Comparing and Contrasting Study Implications with the Literature Review Findings

In comparison to these findings, the chapter 2 literature review revealed no literary source treating specifically the holistic and humanistic approach and perspective to leadership. This approach is however, very strongly influenced and supported by the purported elements and characteristics of other values-based leadership approaches such as Servant Leadership and Transformational Leadership. The overall concept of these two leadership styles does embrace the broad and general theory of a holistic and humanistic approach to leadership. This is so because a leader who practices servant leadership, transformational leadership, and service to others does so out of care and concern for the whole person as opposed to just the worker/follower.

These leadership styles help bring to bear the weight and importance of the leader's guiding and influential values. At the same time, the situational and participative leadership styles discussed in the literature review bring balance to the leader's approach and influence over subordinates by allowing the leader to move among a range of other methods as the situation warrants. The study leaders who adopted a holistic and humanistic approach to leadership often demonstrated and professed situational and participative leadership styles discussed in the literature review sources.

The study also found that, as often stated by the participants, an urgent need for discipline, expedience, or decision making may require the leader to inject authoritative or directive elements into the leadership context tempered by appropriate humanistic elements as required. This corresponds with the literature review findings identifying authoritative and directive leadership as styles often identified with the military. The foregoing concepts are evident in the data and play an overwhelming role in the priority of leadership interactions resulting in successful military leaders of the classic, historical and contemporary eras discussed in the literature review.

Based upon the emergent theory, successful military leadership is grounded in a purely holistic and humanistic values-based approach focused on people and recognized as the impetus moving the organization toward its mission. The human element of the organization becomes the most influential element with the technical and mission-oriented elements in supporting roles as the organization focuses on its purpose, goals, and mission. Data indicated that this humanistic and holistic approach to leadership was universally applicable, adaptable, and effective, regardless of the type of organization, with outlying considerations, and adjustments in means and methods as required.

The Kouzes and Posner (2007) concept of exemplary leadership discussed in the literature review section was evident throughout the present research study. Each of the five identified exemplary practices represented practices of the study participants. The concepts of encouraging the heart and enabling others to act can be linked to the idea of a holistic and humanistic attitude about leadership because people in the organization are a prime consideration. Leading by example is considered the most important military principle (Bantu-Gomez 2004; Shriberg et al. 2002). Of the five leadership practices, modeling the way was the most frequently mentioned. Fourteen of the 16 participants (all eight primary participants and six of the eight secondary participants) discussed the importance and the frequent use of this practice as a means of inspiring and leading followers.

A Holistic and Humanistic Values-Based Leadership Model

The goal of the research study was to create a theoretical model grounded in the data and emerging from an exploration of the specific values that influence and guide the style and practices of successful military leaders. The model resulting from the study reveals the values proclaimed and professed by successful military leaders along with the origin of exemplary leadership styles and preferences. The model is intended to depict four ideas that answer the research questions: (a) the values to which the participants in the study ascribed (the first research question). The model depicts (b) ways in which the participants put the values into practice (the second research question) and (c) the challenges the leaders faced and ways they overcame leadership challenges (the third research question). Finally, the model demonstrates (d) the existing theoretical leadership styles accounting for or explaining successful military leadership (the fourth research question).

According to the analysis of the study results, based on the values mentioned, the leaders were overwhelmingly and primarily guided by values that emerge from embracing a holistic and humanistic approach to leadership. The model depicts the origin of the values (the foundation); the values (RQ1) and most prominent and over-riding value from which the others seem to emanate; and the actions, practices, and behaviors reflective of those values (RQ2). The model also depicts the strategies for overcoming challenges (RQ3); existing leadership models and theories contributing to military leadership success; and organizational output.

The foundation for successful leadership is represented in the model by the values-based holistic and humanistic approach that eventually aligns theory and practice, meaning the leader sees and approaches leadership from a holistic and humanistic perspective. This perspective reflects upon the values of the leader as revealed in personal actions, practices, and behaviors, and is also exemplified in the predominance of the leader's intellect over emotions (*the McMichael Rule*.) From this foundation, the leadership values emerge beginning with the most prominent— care and love.

Holistic and Humanistic Values-Based Leadership Theory
The theory includes the values that are the underlying determinants of success. The yellow on the diagram represents the values, and the theory that personal value systems, once internalized whether consciously or subconsciously, form the foundation and establish the criteria that guide a person's actions (Bruno & Lay 2006).

The care value   successful leaders care about followers. The most frequently mentioned value was that of care, which the participants indicated came from love of people which emerged from a holistic and humanistic foundation (depicted at the base of the diagram). From this value, all the other values seemed to emerge. The values were the main focus of the study, indicated in yellow on the working diagram. The people of the organization are central to this theme and are depicted as being immediately surrounded by the leader's care values.

Other values categories. All the other values categories revealed in the study emanate from the core of the diagram up through the arrows to connect with and be released into the organizational culture as biproducts of the leader's caring nature.

Holistic and Humanistic Values-Based Leadership Practice
For leadership success, theory must be aligned with practice. A positive organizational culture results when theory and practice aligns, as shown in the top portion of the diagram. The values are then demonstrated by the actions, practices, and behaviors of the leaders (represented in

green) as well as in the way the leader faces and responds to organizational challenges (represented in pink.) The theory becomes practice at this level. Practice involves the actions, practices, and behaviors used when facing organizational challenges.

Actions practices and behaviors. The second research question pertained to the actions, practices, and behaviors stemming from the values — how the values were actually put into practice. The participants were asked to cite specific instances that indicated how they aligned their proclaimed leadership values and theory with actual practice. On the diagram, actions, practices, and behaviors (Research Question 2) were color-coded green. The prominent themes included using self-control or discipline; getting to know subordinates and relating to them; and modeling the way – the most cited practice.

Overcoming organizational challenges. The third research question pertained to how the leaders met and overcame leadership challenges, color coded pink on the model. The participants most frequently cited the practice of exercising intellect over emotions, gathering the facts before decision making when possible, and the use of consultation in decision making and taking action.

Contribution of Existing Leadership Styles to Holistic and Humanistic Values-based Leadership
The fourth research question asked about the leadership styles accounting and explaining successful military leadership. The participants were asked which existing styles they ascribe to and used successfully. Four styles were evident by either the express claims of the leaders, or by the characteristics they exhibited based on their responses to the protocol questions. This information is shown in blue on the model diagram. These styles are also important as they provide a valuable contribution to the concept of leadership success as revealed by the participants in the study. The four styles, including servant leadership, participative leadership, transformational leadership, and situational leadership, are also depicted in the diagram as separate but aligning entities or factors.

Output of Successful holistic and Humanistic Values-based Leadership

The extreme top of the diagram represents how the organizational members perpetuate and emulate the leaders' values in their own personal and professional lives and, in doing so, effect and bringing about successful leadership and mission accomplishment. The study results supported the position that organizational members admire and are highly influenced by successful charismatic leadership. Once influenced by successful leadership, organizational members often go on to imitate and eventually demonstrate and hold the same values as their leaders, thus perpetuating and proliferating the values and the success in much the same way as children emulate the values of their parents.

Recommendations

Build a Foundation for Successful Leadership

An all-encompassing concept grounded in and emerging from the data showed that leaders who aspire to excellence and success should first recognize the necessity of taking a holistic and humanistic approach to inspiring and influencing followers. This is the foundation of successful, values-based, leadership. The holistic approach means the leader understands that the follower must learn to function effectively in both the military environment and the civilian environment and subsequently prepares followers for both. A one-dimensional approach to leadership would impose a disservice upon followers and could hamper their ability to succeed in a post-military environment.

A humanistic approach means the leader must demonstrate care, compassion and concern for subordinates and treat them with dignity and respect. The value of organizational members must be affirmed genuinely and constantly, and the leader must demonstrate care and deliberate personal interest in individual members by setting the example, getting to know them, learning how to relate to them, and remaining relevant. When the human element becomes the leading consideration in the organization, leaders will find that embracing the values of successful leaders naturally follows. Good leadership springs from the concept of treating others the way you would like to be treated–with care, compassion, consideration, dignity, and respect.

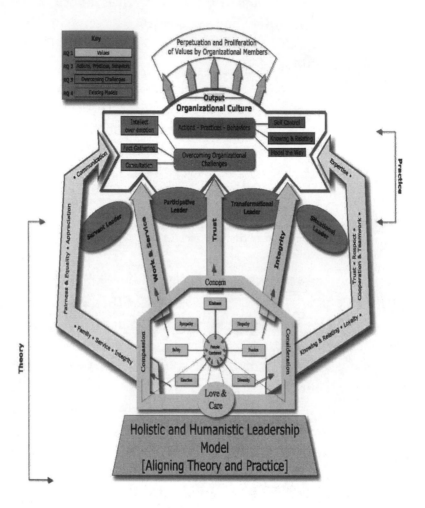

Figure 3. Holistic and humanistic values-based leadership model (aligning theory and practice).

Embrace Corps Values

Sincerely embracing core values ensures success as a military leader. The U.S. military services' core values support this notion. Core values may be those learned at home and practiced as a matter of family tradition and upbringing or those learned and embraced in a professional setting such as the military. Each participant in the present study embraced the core values of specific origins. The seven U.S. Army core values are loyalty, duty, respect, selfless service, honor, integrity, and personal courage. The U.S. Marines and U.S. Navy core values are honor, courage, and commitment. The U.S. Air Force core values are integrity first, service before self, and excellence in all we do. These combined ten values spring from the holistic and humanistic approach to leadership. Study participants also emphasized that early upbringing and traditional family learned values highly influenced their commitment to values-based leadership in their profession as military leaders.

Perpetuate and Emulate Successful Leadership

Successful military leaders perpetuate and emulate organizational and professional leadership in their organization by modeling the way and setting the example, demonstrating in their actions, practices, and behaviors the values they profess. The leaders also face and overcome significant challenges to the benefit, growth, and development of followers while demonstrating technical and tactical excellence and proficiency and embracing successful existing leadership styles and models. Once influenced by successful leadership, organizational members often go on to imitate and eventually demonstrate and hold the same values as their leaders, emulating the values and the success in much the same way as children pass on the values of their parents.

Limitations

When small and unique samples, such as those used in the current study, are used, the results of the study may not be applicable beyond the study sample. A discussion of the limitations will help highlight for the consumer any possible errors or difficulties in interpretation that pertain to the study. As previously noted such limitations are not always apparent at the beginning of the study and may only emerge as the study progresses. The purpose of presenting the limitations is merely to aid the research consumer in his or her interpretation and understanding of the results and how they can be best applied, not to offer alibis or excuses. The present study was limited by certain problems, qualifications, weaknesses, and reservations discussed below.

Limiting Problems Encountered

The unavailability and inaccessibility of an adequate number of participants due to the geographic location of the study was considered a problem limiting the present study. Because the participants' availability could not be controlled, only those individuals who were available and accessible were asked to participate in the study. The fact that the majority of the participants were locally based may have had some known or unknown impact on the results of the study. There was also no guarantee that those participants available at the beginning of the study (especially active duty military personnel) would continue to be available for the duration of the study. This particular issue affected the study only administratively in that an alternate participant had to be solicited, scheduled for the interviews, and interviewed. No other problems limited the study with any possible effect on the findings.

Limiting Qualifications

In research studies involving interviews or any other type of participant responses, a lack of candor in the participants' responses could present qualifications that affect the accuracy and the usefulness of the study results for the research consumer. The use of secondary participants' corroborative statements during the interviews helped to satisfactorily diminish this possibility. Encouraging the participants to be forthright in their responses and explaining the importance of candid responses to the effectiveness of the study may also have helped to diminish the possibility of less than candid responses. The research validity and reliability were not believed to have been compromised by lack of candor on the part of the participants.

Limiting Weaknesses

As noted earlier, the study results are expected to be capable of broad generalization to all branches of the United States military. The only caveat would concern certain training and operational procedures and references to such that may be unique to a particular branch due to differing service mandates and missions. Any such instances encountered in the study were negligible and non-influential on the results of the study and had no weakening effect because the study involved leadership values as opposed to technical matters.

Reservations Related to the Research

The number of participants was restricted due to the purposive sampling requirement. Because of the small number of individuals holding a few unique billets within the military command structure, the participants' experiences may not be correlated with those of the entire represented population. Because the study was based on the experiences of a few senior leaders, logic would dictate that the resulting model may not be effectively applied to junior or subordinate leaders. This observation is not expected to affect the use of the resulting model. The restriction to this small and unique group of senior leaders could also be considered a benefit because it provides the opportunity for junior leaders to learn from the experiences of successful senior leaders for present or future application.

Researcher Bias as a Limiting Factor

Researcher bias also can be considered a limiting factor in the collection and analysis of data. The researcher is the primary instrument in qualitative studies. Researcher bias may have been unintentionally present in the research study because the study was focused on military leaders and was conducted by a military leader. This situation is not expected to affect the study findings in any way because the theory derived was an emergent one, grounded in, and arising from the data itself, and not from the interviewer's personal concepts or notions.

Limitations Related to the Research design

Another issue that may limit the research findings and the use of the resulting model is a recognized limitation of the grounded theory design itself. Because the grounded theory research design often requires an extensive amount of time, systematic, in-depth, analytical procedures for data analysis are often avoided. Researchers often resort to mere descriptions as opposed to engaging in detailed analysis in formulating conclusions. The detailed step-by-step explanation of how the offered theoretical insights and the resulting model were developed in the present research study provides consumers with certainty concerning the credibility and reliability of this source.

Suggestions for Further Research

In accordance with the concept of purposive sampling, certain participants were identified and selected for this qualitative study based on the study purpose (Cooper & Schindler 2006). The purposive selection of this limited population emerged as a result of the unique billet held by the leaders, the leaders' successful military leadership careers, and the relationship and acquaintance of the secondary subjects to the leader. The assertion concerning the success, accomplishments, and qualities of the participants was achievement of the rank and position held, third-party testament, and the documented and chronicled proof of success and achievements of the leaders as evidenced in personal biographies, and other artifacts collected during for the study.

These concepts and procedures helped to satisfy the research questions and identify the values professed and ascribed to by successful military leaders as defined in the study. The study findings supported the suspicion that there may be no shortage of successful military leaders–those achieving the highest rank of their respective military services (Level E-9). A recommendation for further study would be to research the values that guide and influence the style and practices of exceptional military leaders rather than just those considered successful.

Exceptionalism is a more subjective study concept, requiring the researcher to have prior personal knowledge of the participants rather than mere suspicion concerning the participants' possession of the criteria matching the goals of the study. The researcher may develop a set of concrete criteria to determine whether or not exceptional leadership exists. Another process would be to rely upon purely qualitative and subjective means not only in the collection and interpretation of data but also in the sample selection process. The researcher, by virtue of human reasoning capabilities, becomes a valuable research tool not only during the data collection and evaluation phases of the research but also in the early purposive sampling stages.

Summary

The purpose of the present qualitative grounded theory research was to create a model based on the exploration of the values that guide and influence the style and practices of successful military leaders. The study was designed to focus on a group of eight military leaders, two from each of the four U.S. military branches. One female leader was included in the group. Each leader must have achieved the rank of E-9 and be either currently serving on active duty or retired from the military. The study also incorporated the opinions of peers, followers, and superior ranking personnel or mentors of the participants. These secondary participants were intended to corroborate and support the claim made by the primary participants concerning their values and leadership styles.

The pilot study used validated the interview questions, structure and process. The pilot study was conducted in accordance with the procedures specified in Appendix H. More than 200 values emerged from the data collected from all the participants combined. Once integrated and reduced to a manageable size, the data revealed 21 values categories comprising all the values in answer to the overall research question. The top 21 recurring values included those values that can be described as holistic and humanistic values focused on the benefit of the followers, including care, service to others, integrity, loyalty, honor and respects, and so forth.

The values were corroborated, using anecdotes providing specific and citable actions, practices, and behaviors (Research Question 2) of the participants concurrent with their professed values. Secondary participant data and artifacts supplemented and enhanced the claims of the participants. Artifacts took the form of biographies, Internet articles written by or about the participants, and books written by participants. The data from the artifacts were integrated with the data of the primary participants.

The answers to Research Question 3 revealed how the leaders responded when confronted with organizational or personal challenges. Participants were asked to describe the most significant organizational challenge of their leadership career, and to share how they confronted and dealt with the challenge, and provide advice to others with successful leadership aspirations. The participants shared the importance of exercising "intellect over emotions" (as stated by one participant) with emphasis on refraining from making uninformed and spontaneous decisions, and instead exercising discipline, control, calmness, and intellect. The data responding to Research Question 4 indicated that successful military leaders use the servant leadership, transformational leadership, participative decision making, and situational leadership models and styles.

Conclusions

The findings revealed prominent themes related to each of the four research questions. The themes included (a) Successful leaders care about followers, (b) Successful leaders practice their values, (c) Successful leaders face challenges with intellect over emotions, and (d) Successful leaders embrace or incorporate existing leadership styles and models into their own leadership styles. The first recommendation is for military leaders to build a foundation for successful military leadership based on holistic and humanistic leadership practices. The second recommendation is for leaders to embrace core personal and professional values and facilitate the perpetuation and proliferation of meaningful core values in the organization.

The purpose of the qualitative grounded theory research was to create a model based on the exploration of the values that guide and influence the style and practices of successful military leaders. The study results supported the conclusion that successful leadership for the 21st century military must take a holistic and humanistic values-based approach. By embracing and exercising the values revealed by the study, military leaders can respond to the professional and personal needs of followers in such a manner as to preserve human dignity and respect and at the same time capturing the loyalty, respect and obedience of followers.

Based on the study, a Holistic and Humanistic Values-based leadership model was created and described. The model is expected to meet leadership training goals of developing a force committed to moral and ethical values while accomplishing the unique missions of a 21st century military force. The concept is that of a people–centered organization in which the most important element in the organization is the human one.

The study results have the potential of affecting future leadership perspectives not just in large military organizations but also in organizations of all types and sizes. The common denominator in any successful organization is the human element. The people-centered values revealed in the research, if embraced, practiced, and leveraged effectively, will consistently yield favorable and successful results, regardless of the leadership or follower demographics.

Most important is the fact that every leader's chief concern is to ensure not just the fair, equitable, and just treatment of all followers, but also to exercise dignity and respect where each follower is concerned. Showing dignity and respect demonstrates care and love for people and ensures a holistic and humanistic approach to leadership. This concept, in turn, produces success on the part of the leader as the leader's values are perpetuated and proliferated in organizational members, resulting in organizational and leadership success.

REFERENCES

Abrashoff, M. D. (2001). Retention through redemption. *Harvard Business Review*, 79(2), 136-141. Retrieved April 15, 2007, from EBSCOhost database.

Ackmann, M. (2003). *Restricting women's military roles hurts all.* Retrieved March 9, 2008, from Mount Holyoke College Web site: http://www.mtholyoke.edu/offices/ comm/oped/Military.shtml

Advameg. (2009). Ethics. *Reference for business: Encyclopedia of business (2nd ed.).* Retrieved December 21, 2009, from http://www.referenceforbusiness.com /management/Em-Emp/Ethics.html

Air Force Doctrine Document 1-1. (2006). *Leadership and force development.* Retrieved June 17, 2009, from http://www.dtic.mil/doctrine/jel/service_pubs/afdd1_1.pdf

Answers Corporation. (2009). *Joint Chiefs of Staff.* Retrieved May 25, 2009, from http://www.answers.com/topic/joint-chiefs-of-staff#Current_Joint_Chiefs_of_Staff

ArmyStudyGuide. (2008). *Army leadership: Doctrine and the new FM 22-100.* Retrieved January 10, 2009, from http://www.armystudyguide.com/content/ army_board_study_guide_topics/ Leadership/army-leadership-doctrine-.shtml

Avishag, G. (2006). "Purity of arms," "preemptive war," and "selective targeting" in the context of terrorism. *Studies in Conflict & Terrorism*, 29, 493-508. Retrieved February 6, 2009, from EBSCOhost database.

Ayre, M. (2003). What is statistics, population, sample, variables? *Overview of statistical concepts and terms.* Retrieved February 2, 2008, from Seton Hall University Web site: http://academic.shu.edu/eop/worksheets/exac2126/what%20is% 20statistics1203.doc

Bailey, T. M. (2006). Non-combatants in the long war: The end of innocence. *Storming Media Pentagon Reports* [Electronic version]. Retrieved from http://www.stormingmedia.us/ 20/2033/A203364.html?searchTerms=Law—of—Armed—Conflict

Ballard, M. B. (2005). *U. S. Grant: The making of a general, 1861-1863.* Lanham, MD: Rowman & Littlefield.

Bamberg, R., Akroyd, D., & Moore, T. M. (2008). Factors that impact clinical scientist commitment to their work organizations. *Clinical Laboratory Science*, 21(3), 167. Retrieved January 31, 2009, from ProQuest database.

Bantu-Gomez, M. B. (2004). Great leaders teach exemplary followership and serve as servant leaders. *Journal of American Academy of Business, Cambridge*, 4(1/2), 143-151. Retrieved June 24, 2009, from EBSCOhost database.

Barbuto, J. E., & Wheeler, D. W. (2007). *Becoming a servant leader: Do you have what it takes?* University of Nebraska-Lincoln Extension, Institute of Agriculture and Natural Sciences. Retrieved October 13, 2008, from http://www.ianrpubs.unl.edu/epublic/live/g1481/build/g1481.pdf

Barbuto, J. E. (2005). Motivation and transactional, charismatic, and transformational leadership: A test of antecedents. *Journal of Leadership & Organizational Studies, 11*(4), 26-40. Retrieved June 24, 2009, from EBSCOhost database.

Baron, M. A. (2009). *Guidelines for writing research proposals and dissertations.* Retrieved June 11, 2009, from http://www.usd.edu/edad/dissertation_guide. html#CHAPTER 1

Bass, B. M. (1990). From transactional to transformational leadership: Learning to share the vision. *Organizational Dynamics, 18*(3), 19-31. Retrieved June 24, 2009, from EBSCOhost database.

Bass, B. M. (1996). *Transformational leadership: Industrial, military, and educational impact.* Mahwah, NJ: Erlbaum.

Bass, B. M. (1999). Two decades of research and development in transformational leadership. *European Journal of Work & Organizational Psychology, 8*(1), 9–32. Retrieved June 24, 2009, from EBSCOhost database.

Bass, B. M., Avolio, B. J., Jung, D. I., & Berson, Y. (2003). Predicting unit performance by assessing transformational and transactional leadership. *Journal of Applied Psychology, 88*(2), 207-218. Retrieved August 31, 2007, from http://www.apa.org/journals/releases/apl882207.pdf

Baum, D. (2005). Battle lessons. *New Yorker, 80*(43), 42–48. Retrieved February 21, 2008, from EBSCOhost database.

Beatty, J. (2007, March 22). The politics of war. *TheAtlantic.* Retrieved August 26, 2007, from http://www.theatlantic.com/doc/200703u/us-army

Berg, K. E., & Latin, K. W. (2007). *Essentials of research methods in health, physical education, exercise science, and recreation.* Philadelphia, PA: Lippincott, Williams, & Wilkins.

Bitsch, V. (2005). Qualitative research: A grounded theory example and evaluation criteria. *Journal of Agribusiness, 23*(1). Retrieved July17, 2009, from http://www.agecon.uga.edu/~jab/Library/S05-05.pdf

Blake, R. R., & Mouton, J. S. (1985). *The managerial grid III: The key to leadership excellence.* Houston, TX: Gulf.

Bloy, M. (2009). Florence Nightingale (1820–1910). *Literature, history and culture in the age of Victoria.* Retrieved January 2, 2010, from http://www.victorianweb.org/history/crimea/florrie.html

Blum, K. D., & Muirhead, B. (2005). The right horse and harness to pull the carriage: Teaching online doctorate students about literature reviews, qualitative, and quantitative methods that drive the problem. *International Journal of Instructional Technology and Distance Learning, 2*(2). Retrieved July 20, 2006, from http://www.itdl.org/Journal/Feb_05/article03.htm

Boardman, R. (2002). *Unforgettable men in unforgettable times: Stories of honor, courage, commitment, and faith from World War II.* Surprise, AZ: Selah.

Boje, D. (2003). *The leadership box.* Retrieved August 9, 2007, from New Mexico State University Web site at http://cbae.nmsu.edu/~dboje/teaching/338/traits.htm #back_to_universals

Boje, D., & Dennehy, R. (1999*). Managing in a post-modern world* (3rd ed.). Retrieved June 2, 2008, from New Mexico State University Web site at http://cbae.nmsu. edu/~dboje/pages/CHAP5LEA.html

Bolman, L. G., & Deal, T. E. (2008). *Reframing organizations: Artistry, choice and leadership*. San Francisco: Jossey-Bass.

Brown, C. (2001). Ethical theories compared. Retrieved January 14, 2010, from http://www.trinity.edu/cbrown/intro/ethical_theories.html

Brunei Times (2009). Shaping moral values through religion. Retrieved December 21, 2009, from http://www.brudirect.com/index.php/2009111110269/Local-News/shaping-moral-values-through-religion.html

Bruno, L. F., & Lay, E. G. (2006). *Personal values and leadership effectiveness*. Retrieved May 20, 2009, from http://www.g-casa.com/download Bruno _Personal_Values_Leadership.pdf

Burns, B. (2003). National missile defense: A post 9/11 imperative. *Storming Media* (Report No. A359414). Retrieved June 24, 2009, from http://www.stormingmedia.us/35/3594/A359414.html?searchTerms= National~Missile~Defense

Burns, N., & Grove, S. (2005). *The practice of nursing research: Conduct, critique, and utilization* (5th ed.). St. Louis, MO: Elsevier.

Bush, G. W. (2006). State of the union speech. *International Information Programs*. Retrieved February 29, 2008, from http://www.whitehouse.gov/stateoftheunion 2006/

Caldwell, W. B., Murphy, D. M., & Menning, A. (2009). *Learning to leverage new media: The Israeli defense forces in recent conflicts*. U.S. Army War College. Retrieved July 26, 2009, from http://usacac.army.mil/CAC2/MilitaryReview/Archives/English/MilitaryReview_20090630_art004.pdf

Callanan, V. J. (2005). *Types of sampling*. California State University, San Marcos. Retrieved October 17, 2009, from http://www.tardis.ed.ac.uk/~kate/qmcweb/s8.htm

Campbell, A. (2007). *Biography of General George S. Patton, Jr*. Retrieved September 9, 2007, from http://www.generalpatton.com/

Capizzi, J., & Holmes, K. R. (2008). Just war and endgame objectives in Iraq. *The Heritage Foundation*. (Lecture #1081) Retrieved July 22, 2009, from http://www.heritage.org/Research/Thought/hl1081.cfm

Carlson, J. D. (2008). Winning souls and minds: The military's religion problem and the global war on terror. *Journal of Military Ethics*, 7(2), 8-101. Retrieved August 2, 2009, from International Security & Counter-Terrorism Reference Center database.

Carrera, M. L., & Mastaglio, T. W. (2006). Developing tacit knowledge in military leaders through alternate realities: A conceptual framework. *Interservice/Industry Training, Simulation and Education Conference (I/ITSEC) 2006 paper*. Retrieved November 1, 2009. From http://74.125.155.132/search?q=cache:vAadrhkPYCAJ: www.thomascarrera.com/

Carter, P. (2004). The road to Abu Graib: The biggest scandal of the Bush administration began at the top. Retrieved January 17, 2010, from http://www.washingtonmonthly.com/features/2004/0411.carter.html#byline

Cavaleri, D. P. (2005). The law of war: Can 20th –century standards apply to the global war on terrorism? Retrieved October 31, 2009, from http://www-cgsc.army. mil/carl/download/csipubs/cavaleri_law.pdf

Chamberlain, T. (2007). System's dynamics model of Al-Qa'ida and United States competition. *Journal of Homeland Security and Emergency Management*, 4(3), 1- 23. Retrieved April 8, 2008, from EBSCOhost database.

Champion, D. (2006). *Research methods for criminal justice and criminology*. Englewood Cliffs, NJ: Prentice Hall.

Chengming, H. (2007). "A glimpse at *the* cultivation of airmen's core *values* in USAF schools." *Air and Space Power Journal, 21*(4), 55-56. Retrieved September, 26 2009, from International Security & Counter-Terrorism Reference Center (ISCTRC) database.

Citizendium. (2009). Florence Nightingale. Retrieved January 2, 2010, from http://en.citizendium.org/wiki/Florence_Nightingale

Clark, D. R. (2007). Concepts of leadership. *Performance, learning, leadership, and knowledge*. Retrieved August 15, 2007, from http://www.nwlink.com/~donclark/ leader/leadcon.html

Clark, D. R. (2008). *Leadership styles*. Retrieved September 15, 2008, from http://nwlink.com/~donclark/leader/leadstl.html

Clayton, D. (2005). *A call to develop Christ-like leaders*. (Lausanne occasional paper No. 44). Retrieved October 13, 2008, from http://www.lausanne.org/documents /2004forum/LOP41_IG12.pdf

Cohen, D., & Crabtree, B. (2008). *Qualitative research guidelines project*. Retrieved July 17, 2009, from http://www.qualres.org/

Cone, J. D., & Foster, S. L. (2005). *Dissertations and theses from start to finish*. Washington, DC: American Psychological Association.

Connery, W. (2009). *Beloved general of the south*. Retrieved October 31, 2009, from Southern Heritage News and Views Web site: http://shnv.blogspot.com/2009/01 /happy-202nd-birthday-robert-e-lee-1-19.html

Cooper, D. R., & Schindler, P. S. (2006). *Business research methods* (9th ed.). Boston: McGraw Hill Irwin.

Cooperrider, D., & Whitney, D. (2005). *Appreciative inquiry: A positive revolution in change*. San Francisco: Berrett-Koehler.

Cooperrider, D., Whitney, D., & Stavros, J. (2005). *Appreciative inquiry handbook: The first in a series of AI workbooks for leaders of change*. Brunswick, OH: Crown Custom.

Covey, S. R. (1989). *Seven habits of highly effective people*. New York: Simon & Schuster.

Covey, S. R. (2004). *The 8th habit*. New York: Simon & Schuster.

Creswell, J. W. (2005). *Educational research: Planning, conducting, and evaluating quantitative and qualitative research* (2nd ed.). Upper Saddle River, NJ: Prentice Hall.

Creswell, J. W. (2007). *Qualitative inquiry and research design: Choosing among five approaches* (2nd ed.). Thousand Oaks, CA: Sage.

Crossan, M., & Mazutis, D. (2007). Transcendent leadership. *Business Horizons, 51*(2), 131-159. Retrieved January 31, 2009, from ProQuest database.

Darken, R. P., & Sadagic, A. (2006). Combined arms training: Measures and methods for a changing world. *Storming Media Pentagon Reports* (Report No. A903374). Retrieved from http://www.stormingmedia.us/90/9033/A903374.html ?searchTerms=combined~arms~training

Data selection. (n.d.). *Responsible conduct in data management*. Retrieved February 3, 2008, from Northern Illinois University Web site: http://www.niu.edu/rcrportal/ datamanagement/dstopic.html

de Jong, J. H. M. (2007). *Charismatic leadership (Weber)*. Retrieved August 30, 2007, from http://www.12manage.com/methods_weber_charismatic_leadership.html Defense and the National Interest. (2007). *Leadership*. Retrieved June 27, 2008, from http://www.d-n-i.net/dni/people/leadership/

Defense Technical Information Center. (2007). *Strategies against terrorism: Bibliographies*. Scientific and technical information network (STINET). Retrieved March 5, 2008, from http:// stinet.dtic.mil/3

Dent, E. B., Higgins, M. E., & Wharff, D. M. (2005). *Spirituality and leadership: An empirical review of definitions, distinctions, and embedded assumptions.* Retrieved August 4, 2007, from University of North Carolina at Pembroke Web site: http://www.uncp.edu/home/dente/LQPaper.pdf

Denzin, N. K., & Lincoln, Y. S. (2005). *The Sage handbook of qualitative research* (3rd ed.). Thousand Oaks, CA; Sage.

Department of the Army. (2006). *Headquarters, Department of the Army (2006).* FM 6-22 (FM 22-100). Retrieved October 24, 2009, from http://www.fas.org/irp /doddir/army/fm6-22.pdf

Dick, B. (2005). *Grounded theory: A thumbnail sketch.* Retrieved May 21, 2009, from http://www.scu.edu.au/schools/gcm/ar/arp/grounded.html

DiMatteo, B. C. (2007). Quiet leaders learn some service lessons. *Personal Excellence, 12*(1), 14. Retrieved April 15, 2007, from EBSCOhost database.

Dion, M. (2007). *Military ethics and virtues: The attitudes required for a cross-cultural/inter-religious dialogue.* Retrieved February 24, 2008, from United States Air Force Academy Web site: http://www.usafa.edu/isme/ISME07/ Papers/Michal%20Dion%20ReligionMilitary2.doc

Dodd, M. (2004). *Understand leadership before you report it.* Retrieved April 15, 2007, from http://www.military.com/NewContent/0,13190,Defensewatch_032604 _Leadership1,00 .html

Dombeck, M., & Wells-Moran, J. (2006). Values and morals clarification. Retrieved January, 8, 2010, from http://www.mentalhelp.net/poc/view_doc.php?type=doc &id=9795&cn=353

Donahoe, P. (2004). Preparing leaders for nation building. *Military Review.* Retrieved February 23, 2008, from Air University Web site: http://www.au.af.mil/au /awc/awcgate/milreview/don.pdf

Drew, C. T. (2005). *Critical thinking and the development of innovative problem solvers.* Retrieved June 13, 2005, from http://www.dtic.mil/cgi-bin/GetTRDoc?AD =ADA464378&Location= U2&doc=GetTRDoc.pdf

Drucker, P. F. (1967). *The effective executive.* New York: Harper & Rowe. Encyclopedia of Spiritual Knowledge, (n.d.). Ethics. Retrieved December 20, 2009, from http://www.encyclopedia of religion.org/ethics.html#Difference_between _Morals_ and_ Ethics

Estes, K. W. (2008). *Handbook for Marine NCOs* (5th ed.). Annapolis, MD: U.S. Naval Institute Press.

Eyler, L. T., & Jeste, D. V. (2006). Enhancing the informed consent process: A conceptual overview. *Behavioral Sciences & the Law, 24*(4), 553-568. Retrieved June 24, 2009, from EBSCOhost database.

Fatur, R. P. (2005). *Influencing transnational terrorist organizations: Using influence nets to prioritize factors.* Air Force Institute of Technology, Wright-Patterson AFB, School of Engineering and Management. Retrieved March 5, 2008, from http://stinet.dtic.mil/dticrev/BibliographyFall5.html

Fawcett, S. E., Brau, J. C., Rhoads, G. K., Whitlark, D., & Fawcett, A. M. (2008). Spirituality and organizational culture: Cultivating the ABCs of an inspiring workplace. *International Journal of Public Administration, 31*(4), 420-438. Retrieved January 31, 2009, from ProQuest database.

Feminism: Africa and African Diaspora. (2005). In *New dictionary of the history of ideas* (Vol. 2) (1st ed.). Detroit, MI: Scribner. Retrieved February 14, 2009, from http://www.piercecountylibrary.org

Francis, A. J., Sr. (2008). Changes make courses more relevant to GWOT. *Infantry, 97*(5), 13-15.

Retrieved January 31, 2009, from EBSCOhost database.

Fry, J. (Speaker). (2007). *The learning organization and spiritual leadership theory*. [Online audio streaming]. Retrieved August 9, 2007, from http://www.iispiritualleadership.com/index.htm

Fry, L. W., & Matherly, L. L. (2007). Workplace spirituality, spiritual leadership, and performance excellence. In S. G. Rogleberg, (Ed.), *Encyclopedia of industrial and organizational psychology*. San Francisco: Sage. Retrieved September 4, 2009, from http://www.tarleton.edu/~fry/SL-TEncyclepedIOPsyc.pdf

Gerges, F. A. (2004). *U.S. nation-building abroad, part II: Iraqi abuse revelations deepen distrust of US. Yale Center for the Study of Globalization*. Retrieved February 29, 2008, from http://yaleglobal.yale.edu/display.article?id=3993

Glaser, B. G., & Strauss, A. L. (1967). *The discovery of grounded theory: Strategies for qualitative research*. Chicago: Aldine.

Golafshani, N. (2004). *Understanding reliability and validity in qualitative research*. Retrieved October 15, 2008, from http://www.nova.edu/ssss/QR/QR8-4/ golafshani.pdf

Greenleaf, R. K. (1977). *Servant leadership*. Mahwah, NJ: Paulist Press.

Greenleaf, R. K. (1991). *The servant as leader*. Westfield, IN: Robert Greenleaf Center. Greenleaf, R. K., Spears, L. C., & Covey, S. R. (2002). *Servant leadership: A journey into the nature of legitimate power and greatness*. Mahwah, NJ: Paulist Press.

Greenslit, L. P. (2006). Religion and the military: A growing ethical dilemma. *Storming Media Pentagon Reports*. (Report No. A176844). Retrieved June 24, 2009, from http://www.stormingmedia.us/17/1768/A176844.html

Greenwald, G. (2006). Unclaimed territory. Retrieved December 20, 2009, from http://glenngreenwald.blogspot.com/2006/12/winning-hearts-and-minds.html

Grid International. (2009). *The leadership grid*. Retrieved February 25, 2009, from http://www.gridinternational.com/gridtheory.html

Guion, L. A., & Flowers, L. (2008). *Using qualitative research in planning and evaluating extension programs*. Retrieved October 12, 2008, from University of Florida IFAS Extension Web site: http://edis.ifas.ufl.edu/pdffiles/FY/FY39200. pdf

Hancock, B. (2002). *An introduction to qualitative research*. Retrieved May 24, 2009, from http://www.trentrdsu.org.uk/cms/uploads/Qualitative%20Research.pdf

Hartle, A. E. (2007). *Moral issues in military decision making* (2nd ed., rev.). Lawrence: University Press of Kansas.

Helm, A. M. (Ed.). (2006). The law of war in the 21st century: Weaponry and the use of force. *International Law Studies* (Vol. 82). Retrieved March 31, 2009, from http://www.nwc.navy.mil/cnws/ild/documents/Naval%20War%20College%20vol %2082%20.pdf

Hercik, J., Lewis, R., Myler, B., Gouvus, C., Zweig, J., Whitby, A., et al. (2005). Development of a guide to resources on faith-based organizations in criminal justice. Retrieved January 23, 2010, from http://www.ncjrs.gov/pdffiles1 /nij/grants/209350.pdf

Hester, J. P., & Killian, D. R. (2010). The moral foundations of ethical leadership. *Journal of Values-Based Leadership*, *III*(1), 66-76. Retrieved June 35, 3009, from http://www.valuesbased-leadershipjournal.com/assets/docs/Vol3Issue1.pdf

Holdstock, D. (2001). Reacting to terrorism [Editorial]. *British Medical Journal*, *323*(7317), 822. Retrieved July 26, 2009, from ProQuest database.

Hoving, R. (2007). Information technology leadership challenges: Past, present, and future, 24(2), 147-153. Retrieved January 31, 2009, from ProQuest database.

Huddy, L., Feldman, S., Taber, C., & Lahav, G. (2005). Threat, anxiety, and support of antiterrorism policies. *American Journal of Political Science, 49*, 593-608. Retrieved April 26, 2008, from EBSCOhost database

Ibrahim, A. (2008). Military morals. Retrieved January 16, 2010, from http://www. kenyaimagine. com/index2.php?option=com_content&do_pdf=1&id=375

Jandeska, K. E., & Kraimer, M. L. (2005). Women's perceptions of organizational culture, work attitudes, and role-modeling behaviors. *Journal of Managerial Issues, 17*(4), 461-478. Retrieved June 24, 2009, from EBSCOhost database.

Jaszlics, S. L., Sanders, S., & Culkin, A. (2006). *Obstacle marking and vehicle guidance science and technology objective (OMVG-STO) augmented reality for enhanced command and control and mobility.* Defense Technical Information Center. Retrieved June 26, 2008, from http://stinet.dtic. mil/oai/oai?verb= getRecord&metadataPrefix=html&identifier=ADA457374

Jensen, R. (2003). Patriotism's bad idea at a dangerous time. *Peace Review, 15*, 389-396. Retrieved April 26, 2008, from EBSCOhost database.

Johnson, J. L., & Hill, W. R. (2009). Personality traits and military leadership. *Individual Differences Research 2009, 7*(1), 1-13. Retrieved June 24, 2009, from EBSCOhost database.

Joseph, P. T. (2003). Leadership styles and competencies: An exploratory study. *Journal of the Academy of Business and Economics.* Retrieved August 15, 2008, from http://findarticles.com/p/articles/mi_m0OGT/is_2_2/ai_113563661

Kagan, F. W. (2006). *Why military history matters.* Retrieved October 11, 2008, from http://www.campbell.edu/faculty/Slattery/WhyStudyMilitaryHistory.pdf

Kalb, M. (2003). Dissent: Public opinion, media reaction. *Nieman Foundation for Journalism.* Retrieved February 24, 2008, from http://www.nieman.harvard.edu/

Kamil, M. (2004). The current state of quantitative research. *Reading Research Quarterly, 39*(1), 100-107. Retrieved June 24, 2009, from EBSCOhost database.

Kelly, M. (2010). Theodore Roosevelt–twenty-sixth president of the United States. Retrieved January 31, 2010, from http://americanhistory.about.com/od /troosevelt/p/ptroosevelt.htm

Karp, T., & Johannessen, J-A. (2010). Turning the right to lead in defining moments: The act of taking leadership. *Journal of Values-Based Leadership, III*(1), 48-65. Retrieved June 24, 2009, from http://www.valuesbasedleadershipjournal. com/assets/docs/Vol3Issue1.pdf

Kincaid, C. (2004). Moral corruption infects the military. Retrieved January 16, 2010, from http://www.aim.org/media-monitor/moral-corruption-infects-the-military/

Kleinman, C. (2004). The relationship between managerial leadership behaviors and nursing staff retention. *Hospital Topics: Research and Perspectives on Healthcare, 82*(4), 2-9. Retrieved June 24, 2009, from EBSCOhost database.

Knapp, M. L. (2009). *Aging in place in suburbia: A qualitative study of older women.* (Doctoral dissertation, Antioch University, 2008). *Dissertation Abstracts International.* (UMI No. 3350674)

Kohn, R. H. (2008). Coming soon: A crisis in civil-military relations. *World Affairs, 170*(3), 69-80. Retrieved June 24, 2009, from EBSCOhost database.

Kohn, L. T. (1997). *Methods in case study analysis.* Retrieved February 3, 2008, from Center for Studying Health System Change Web site: http://www.hschange.org /CONTENT/158/158.pdf

Kondrasuk, J. N., Bailey, D., & Sheeks, M. (2005). Leadership in the 21st century: Understanding global terrorism. *Employee Responsibilities and Rights Journal, 17*(4), 263-279. Retrieved June 24, 2009, from EBSCOhost database.

Kouzes, J., & Posner, B. (2007). *The leadership challenge*. San Francisco: Jossey Bass.

Krulak, C. (2000). Remarks at JSCOPE 2000. *Joint Services Conference on Professional Ethics*. Retrieved June 5, 2008, from http://www.usna63.org/tradition/history/EthicsKrulak.html

Lambert, M. T. (2006). Aripiprazole in the management of post-traumatic stress disorder symptoms in returning Global War on Terrorism veterans. *International Clinical Psychopharmacology Journal, 21*(3), 185-187. Retrieved September 7, 2009, from http://www.ncbi.nlm.nih.gov/pubmed/16528142

Latour, S. M., & Rast, V. J. (2004). *Dynamic followership: The prerequisite for effective leadership*. Retrieved March 31, 2009, from http://www.airpower.maxwell.af .mil/airchronicles/apj/apj04 /win04/latour.html

Leader to Leader Institute. (2007). Be, know, do. *Leader to Leader Journal*, (26). Retrieved October 24, 2009, from http://www.leadertoleader.org/knowledgecenter /journal.aspx?ArticleID=126

Leader to Leader Institute. (2007). *Publications*. Retrieved March 24, 2008, from http://www.pfdf .org/

Leadership. (1980). *Marine Corps manual*. Retrieved August 12, 2007, from http://www.usmc.mil/ directiv.nsf/

Leedy, P. D., & Ormrod, J. E. (2005). *Practical research: Planning and design* (8th ed.). Upper Saddle River, NJ: Prentice Hall.

Leedy, P. D., & Ormrod, J. E. (2008). *Practical research: Planning and design* (8th ed.). Upper Saddle River, NJ: Pearson Prentice Hall.

Lehman, P. R. (2004). Embedded media and the operational commander. *Storming Media Pentagon Reports*. (Report No. A987224). Retrieved July 5, 2008, from http://www.stormingmedia.us/ 98/9872/A987224.html?searchTerms=Embedded—Media—and—the—Operational—Commander

Le Pla, A. M., & Roberts, H. (2004). *Legitimate leadership: An inquiry into the principles of engendering commitment*. Retrieved March 8, 2008, from http://www.cmsconsult.co.uk/downloads/LEGITIMATE%20LEADERSHIP%20PHASE %202%20REPORT.pdf

Levine, J. M., & Moreland, R. L. (2006). *Small groups: Key readings*. New York: Psychology Press.

Levitt, H. M., Neimeyer, R. A., & Williams, D. C. (2005). Rules vs. principles in psychotherapy: Implications of the quest for universal guidelines in the movement for empirically supported treatments. *Journal of Contemporary Psychology, 35*(1), 117–129. Retrieved September 7, 2008, from ProQuest database.

Lincoln, Y. S., & Guba, E. G. (1985). *Naturalistic inquiry*. Newbury Park, CA: Sage.

Lock, G. (2003). Living, valuing, and sharing: A case study of retaining IT professionals in the British Columbia public service. *Career Development International, 8*(3), 152-158. Retrieved June 24, 2009, from EBSCOhost database.

Locke, K. (2001). *Grounded theory in management research*. Thousand Oaks, CA: Sage.

Long Thompson, J. (2010). introducing ethics legislation: The courage to lead after 200 years of silence. *Journal of Values-Based Leadership, III*(1), 11-40. Retrieved June 24, 3009, from http://www.valuesbasedleadershipjournal.com/assets/docs /Vol3Issue1.pdf

Looney, J. D. (2004). Military leadership evaluations: Effects of sex, leadership style, and gender-role attitudes. *Storming Media Pentagon Reports* (Report No. A993524). Retrieved September 9, 2008, from http://www.stormingmedia.us/99/9935 /A993524.html

Looney, J. D., Kurpius, S. E. R., & Lucart, L. (2004). Military leadership evaluations effects of evaluator sex, leader sex, and gender role attitudes. *Consulting Psychology Journal: Practice and Research, 1065-9293, 56*(2), 104-118. Retrieved September 9, 2008, from EBSCOhost database.

Looper, J. (2007). *A personal code of values: What are values and how do you find them?* Retrieved December 20, 2009, from http://self-awareness.suite101. com/article.cfm/a_personal_code_of_values

Love. (2010). *Merriam-Webster Online Dictionary*. Retrieved August 20, 2010, from http://www.merriam-webster.com/dictionary/love

Mack, N., Woodsong, C., MacQueen, K. M., Guest, G., & Namey, E. (2005). *Qualitative research methods: A data collector's field guide*. Retrieved December 28, 2007, from Family Health International Web site: http://www.fhi.org/NR/rdonlyres

Marine Corps leadership traits. (2007). Retrieved January 20, 2008, from Air University, Center for Strategic Leadership Studies Web site: http://www.au.af.mil/au/awc /awcgate/usmc/leadership_traits.htm

Marshall, C., & Rossman, G. B. (2006). *Designing qualitative research* (4th ed.). Thousand Oaks, CA: Sage.

Matthew, C. T., Cianciola, A. T., & Sternberg, R. J. (2005). *Developing effective military leaders: Facilitating the acquisition of experience-based tacit knowledge*. United States Army Research Institute for the Behavioral and Social Sciences. Retrieved April 26, 2008, from Air University Web site: http://www.au.af.mil/au/awc awcgate/army/tr1161.pdf

Maxwell, J. C. (2007). *The 21 irrefutable laws of leadership: Follow them and people will follow you*. Nashville, TN: Thomas Nelson.

McCormick, B., & Davenport, D. (2003). *Shepherd leadership: Wisdom for leaders from Psalm 23*. Somerset, NJ: Wiley.

McCrimmon, M. (2007). What is autocratic leadership? How command and control is giving way to thought leadership. Retrieved September 21, 2009, from http://businessmanagement. suite101.com/article.cfm/what_is_autocratic _leadership

McGill, S. A. (2009). *Alexander the Great*. Retrieved January 31, 2009, from EBSCOhost database

McLane, B. R. (2004). Reporting from the sandstorm: An appraisal of embedding. *Parameters*, U. S. Army War College. Retrieved March 5, 2008, from http://carlisle-www.army.mil/usawc/Parameters/04spring/mclane.htm

McMichael, A. L. (2008). *Leadership: Achieving life-changing success from within*. New York: Simon & Schuster.

MCWP 6-11. (2002). Leading marines. Retrieved January 14, 2010, from http://www.au.af.mil/au/awc/awcgate/usmc/mcwp611.pdf

Menking, H. C. (2003). *Programa liderazgo educativo, Ecuador: A qualitative case study of an experiment in transformational leadership, education, and community development*. (Doctoral dissertation, University of New Mexico, Albuquerque, United States—New Mexico). Retrieved February 8, 2008, from ProQuest Dissertations and Theses database. (AAT 3080545)

Micewski, E. R. (2008). *Military morals and societal values–Military virtues versus bureaucratic reality*. Retrieved January 17, 2010, from http://www.bmlv.gv. at/pdf_pool/publikationen /08_cma_04_mic.pdf

Mills, D. Q. (2005). Asian and American leadership styles: How are they unique? *Working Knowledge for Business Leaders*. Retrieved April 1, 2008, from http://hbswk.hbs.edu/item/4869.html

Mills, G. E. (2007). *Action research: A guide for the teacher researcher* (3rd ed.). Englewood Cliffs,

NJ: Prentice Hall.

Minaudo, M. F. (2009, May 4). Design: The future of planning? *Storming Media Pentagon Reports* (Report No. A528994). Retrieved September 7, 2010, from http://www.stormingmedia.us/52/5289/A528994.html

Moutet, J. (2004). *Leadership theory*. Retrieved August 9, 2007, from http://www.apparelwarehousing.com/Leadership.htm

Mueller-Hansen, R. A., White, S. S., Dorsey, D. W., & Pulakos, E. D. (2005). Training adaptable leaders: Lessons from research and practice. *Storming Media Pentagon Reports* (Report No. A931044). Retrieved September 7, 2010, from http://www.stormingmedia.us/93/9310/A931044.html?searchTerms =Training~adaptable~leaders

Murray, T. M. (2008). *A grounded theory of U.S. army installation realignment and closure leadership characteristics.* (Doctoral dissertation, University of Phoenix, United States—Arizona). ProQuest Dissertations and Theses database. (AAT 3326209)

Muskoff, J. A. (2006). Integrity failures: A strategic leader problem. *Storming Media Pentagon Reports* (Report No. A046944). Retrieved September 8, 2010, from http://www.stormingmedia.us/04/0469/A046944. html?searchTerms=Integrity~ Failures

Myarmedforces Military Friends Network. (2009). *Sergeant Major of the Marine Corps*. Retrieved July 17, 2009, from http://www.myarmedforces.com/rank-81 Sergeant_Major_Of_The_Marine_Corps

Neill, J. (2007). *Qualitative versus quantitative research: Key points in a classic debate*. Retrieved January 19, 2008, from http://wilderdom.com/research/ QualitativeVersusQuantitativeResearch. html#Features

Nemitz-Mills, P. (1999). *Leadership basics*. Retrieved June 5, 2008, from Eastern Washington University Web site: http://www.cbpa.ewu.edu/~pnemetzmills /326ch14.html

Nordstrom, B. J. (2004). Gustavus II Adolphus (Sweden). Europe, 1450 to 1789. In J. Dewald (Ed.), *Encyclopedia of the early modern world* (pp. 104-105). New York: Scribner. Retrieved May 17, 2008, from http://go.galegroup.com/

North Georgia College and State University. (2004). *Leadership theories*. Retrieved October 13, 2008, from http://www.ngcsu.edu/Ldrship/theory.htm

Oliver Cromwell Association. (2001). *Cromwell: A brief biography*. Retrieved May 20, 2007, from http://www.olivercromwell.org/biography.htm

Parco, J. E., & Fagin, B. S. (2007). The one true religion in the military. *The humanist, 67*(5), 11-18. Retrieved January 31, 2009, from ProQuest database.

Parmley, R. R. (2005). [Review of the book *The handbook of workplace spirituality and organizational performance*]. Retrieved August 9, 2007, from http://www. newwork.com/Pages/Reviews/Books/WorkplacespiritReview%20.html

Parrish, W. H. (2006). International cooperation in combating terrorism. *Journal of the Institute of Justice and International Studies*, 51-69. Retrieved July 26, 2009, from ProQuest database.

Pasquarett, M. (2003, October). *Reporters on the ground: The military and the media's joint experience during operation Iraqi freedom*. Center for Strategic Leadership, Issue Paper, *08-03*. Retrieved September 8, 2010, from http://oai.dtic.mil/oai /oai?verb=getRecord&metadataPrefix=html&identifier=ADA423934

Patton, M. Q. (2002). Qualitative research and evaluation methods. Thousand Oaks, CA: Sage.

Patzer, M. S. (2008). *History and women: Amina of Zaria: 1533–1610*. Retrieved June 13, 2009, from http://www.historyandwomen.com/search?q=Amina+of+Zaria

Pernoud, R. (2003). Joan of Arc, St. *New Catholic encyclopedia* (Vol. 2) (2nd ed.). Detroit, MI: Gale. Retrieved May17, 2008, from http://go.galegroup.com/

Peters, R. (2007). Progress and peril. *Armed Forces Journal*. Retrieved October 11, 2008, from http://www.armedforcesjournal.com/2007/02/2456854

Petrauskaite, A. (2008). Ethics and leadership responsibility. *Osterreichs Bundesheer*. Retrieved March 24, 2008, from http://www.bmlv.gv.at/pdf_pool/publikationen /10_cma_08_elp.pdf

Pfaff, T. (2002). *Virtue ethics and military leadership*. Retrieved April 15, 2007, from Association for Christian Conferences Teaching and Service Web site: http://www.accts.org/ministries/ethics/latvia/Papers/Virtue_ethics.htm

Popper, M., Amit, K., Gal, R., Mishkal-Sinai, M., & Lisak, A. (2007). *The leadership formula*: *P*M*D*. U.S. Army Research Institute for the Behavioral and Social Sciences. Retrieved July 17, 2009, from http://www.hqda.army.mil/ari/pdf /CR2007-10.pdf

Precept for the board to select nominees to be considered as the 15th sergeant major of the Marine Corps. (2003). Manpower Management Promotions Branch, CMC: U.S. Marine Corps.

Prewitt, E. (2004, December 30). *The best leadership style? It all depends*. Retrieved August 15, 2007, from CIO Web site: http://www.cio.com/article/print/1026

Price, R. G. (2004). *History of the separation of church and state in America*. Retrieved April 1, 2008, from National Revolution Web site: http://www.rationalrevolution. net/articles/history_of_the_separation_of_chu.htm

Province, C. M. (2008). *The world's greatest military leaders*. Retrieved September 14, 2008, from The Patton Society Web site: http://www.pattonhq.com /militaryworks/leaderslist.html

Putko, M. M., & Johnson, D. V., II. (2008). *Women in combat compendium*. Retrieved October 17, 2008, from U.S. Army Strategic Studies Institute Web site: http://www.strategicstudiesInstitute.army.mil/pdffiles/PUB830.pdf

Quinn, R. E. (2004). *Building the bridge as you walk on it: A guide for leading change*. San Francisco: Jossey-Bass

Rabinowitz, P., & Berkowitz, B. (2009) *Qualitative methods to assess community issues*. Retrieved June 11, 2009, from http://ctb.ku.edu/en/tablecontents/sub_section _main_1050.htm

Randall, E. W. (2006). *Military leadership: The effect of leader behavior on soldier retention in the Army National Guard*. (Doctoral dissertation, Capella University, United States—Minnesota). Retrieved April 27, 2008, from ProQuest Dissertations and Theses database. (AAT 3215982)

Ready, D. A. (2005). Is your company failing its leaders? *Business Strategy Review, 16*(4), 21-25. Retrieved January 31, 2009, from ProQuest database.

Recovery Nation. (2009). *Recovery workshop: Lesson three. The role of values*. Retrieved July 17, 2009, from http://www.recoverynation.com/recovery /m1w1d3.htm

Reynolds, C. R., Livingston, R. B., & Wilson, V. (2006). Measurement and assessment in education. Upper Saddle River, NJ: Pearson Education.

Rice, K. (2010). U.S. military value system. Retrieved January 14, 2010, from http://ezinearticles .com/?US-Military-Value-System&id=313149

Rice, K. (2005, December 28). *Spiritual shape shifting—Christian leadership in an amoral society*. Retrieved January 23, 2010, from http://ezinearticles.com /?Spiritual-Shape-Shifting—-Christian-Leadership-in-an-Amoral-Society&id =119342

Rivkin, R. S. (2004). *A duty to disobey: The forgotten lessons of My Lai*. Pacific News Service. Retrieved March 5, 2008, from News America Media Web site: http://news.newamericamedia.org/

Ruane, J., & Ramcharan, P. (2006). Grounded theory and membership categorization analysis:

Partner methodologies for establishing social meaning—A research example. *Clinical Effectiveness in Nursing, 9*(3), e308-e316. Retrieved January 25, 2008, from ScienceDirect database.

Ruderman, M. N. (2008). Great expectations: Resolving conflicts of leadership style preferences. *Leadership in Action, 28*(4), 8-12. Retrieved January 31, 2009, from ProQuest database.

Saddler, D. (2007). *A comparison of quantitative and qualitative research terms.* Retrieved September 20, 2009, from http://www.nursingcenter.com/library /journalArticle.asp?Article_ID= 737387

Sampson, H. (2004). Navigating the waves: The usefulness of a pilot in qualitative research. *Qualitative Research, 4*(3), 383-402. Retrieved September 8, 2008, from EBSCOhost database.

Scientific observations. (2008). *Science News, 174*(6), 4-4. Retrieved July 19, 2009, from the Gale Group.

Secretary of the Army. (2006). *A strategic framework: Serving a nation at war.* U.S. Army. Retrieved February 23, 2008, from National Guard Association of the United States Web site: http://www.ngaus.org/

Seidman, I. (2006). *Interviewing as qualitative research: A guide for researchers in education and the social sciences.* New York: Teachers College Press.

Shah, S. K., & Corley, K. G. (2006). Building better theory by bridging the quantitative-qualitative divide. *Journal of Management Studies, 43*(8), 1821-1835. Retrieved June 24, 2009, from EBSCOhost database.

Shank, G. D. (2006). *Qualitative research: A personal skills approach* (2nd ed.). Upper Saddle River, NJ: Prentice Hall.

Shriberg, A., Shriberg, D., & Lloyd, C. (2002). *Practicing leadership: Principles and applications* (2nd ed.). New York: Wiley.

Simon, S. (2003). The new terrorism. *The Brookings Review, 21*(1), 18-25. Retrieved July 26, 2009, from ProQuest database.

Smith, F. W. (2007). [Review of the book *Semper fi: Business leadership the Marine Corps way*]. Retrieved February 21, 2008, from Semperfi consulting Web site: http://www.semperficonsulting.com/reviews.htm

Smith, M. K. (2000). Curriculum theory and practice. *The encyclopaedia of informal education.* Retrieved July 22, 2009, from http://www.infed.org/biblio/b-curric.htm

Smith, W. T., Jr. (2007). *Beyond the drop zone.* Retrieved August 10, 2007, from World Defense Review News Commentary & Analysis Web site: http://worlddefensereview.com/wts012207 .shtml

Smith-Stark, L. (2007). *U. S. military takes Iraq war to YouTube.* Retrieved August 26, 2007, from BBC News Web site: http://news.bbc.co.uk/1/hi/world/americas/ 6639401.stm

Spencer, R. (2007). Believing in the war on terror. *Human Events, 63*(16), 12-12. Retrieved August 4, 2009, from International Security & Counter-Terrorism Reference Center (ISCTRC) database.

Stanford Encyclopedia of Philosophy. (2007). Deontological ethics. Retrieved January 14, 2009, from http://plato.stanford.edu/entries/ethics-deontological/

Starling, J. (2009). *Leadership: The shepherd model.* Retrieved January 8, 2010, from http://committedtotruth.wordpress.com/2009/10/07/leadership-6-the-shepherd-model/

Sterngold, J. (2004). Bush tempers argument for pre-emptive strikes; Experts say Iraq war precludes similar future engagements. *San Francisco Chronicle,* Retrieved July 30, 2009, from International Security & Counter Terrorism Reference Center database.

Steward, J. (2006). *Transformational leadership: An evolving concept explored through the works of Burns, Bass, Avolio, and Leithwood*. Retrieved October 11, 2008, from http://www.umanitoba.ca/publications/cjeap/articles/stewart.html

Strauss, A. (1987). *Qualitative analysis for social scientists*. Cambridge, United Kingdom: University of Cambridge Press.

Strauss, A., & Corbin, J. (1998). *Basics of qualitative research: Techniques and procedures for developing grounded theory* (2nd ed.). Thousand Oaks, CA: Sociology Press.

Suddaby, R. (2006). From the editors: What grounded theory is not. *Academy of Management Journal, 49*, 633-642. Retrieved June 24, 2009, from EBSCOhost database.

Sumner, M., & Niederman, F. (2004). The impact of gender differences on job satisfaction, job turnover, and career experiences of information systems professionals. *Journal of Computer Information Systems, 44*(2), 29-39. Retrieved September 7, 2008, from EBSCOhost database.

Supervielle, M. E. F. (2005). Islam, the law of war, and the U.S. Soldier. *American University International Law Review, 21*(2), 191-219. Retrieved December 20, 2009, from EBSCOhost database.

Swiatek, M. S. (2005, January 27). *The pomo O*. Paper submitted to the Joint Services Conference on Professional Ethics. Retrieved March 2, 2008, from U.S. Air Force Web site: http://www.usafa.edu/isme/JSCOPE05/Swiatek05.html

Taylor, R. L., & Rosenbach, W. E. (2005). *Military leadership. In pursuit of excellence*. (5th ed.). Boulder, CO: Westview Press.

Teddlie, C., & Yu, F. (2007). Mixed methods sampling. A typology with examples. *Journal of Mixed Methods Research, 1*(1), 77-100. Retrieved June 24, 2009, from ERIC database.

Tendai, D. (2006). *Leadership styles that affect performance of subordinates*. Retrieved August 15, 2007, from http://www.ipp.co.tz/ipp/guardian/2006/04/05/63586.html

Testa, A. C., & Coleman, L. M. (2006). Accessing research participants in schools: A case study of UK adolescent sexual health survey. *Health Education Research Theory & Practice, 21*, 518-526. Retrieved December 3, 2008, from http://her.oxfordjournals.org/cgi/reprint/cyh078v1.pdf

Theisen, K. L. (2008). *The war on terror is a war OF terror*. Retrieved April 1, 2009, from http://worldcantwait.net/index

Theros, P. (2003). Ruining the neighborhood: War with Iraq and the neighbors. *Mediterranean Quarterly, 14*(3), 12-24. Retrieved April 26, 2008, from EBSCOhost database.

Thomas, G. (2001). Understanding leadership in the 21st century. Retrieved June 10, 2009, from http://www.leadingtoday.org/Onmag/jan01/leadership12001.htm

Thomsong, S. (2004). *Leadership in the military*. Retrieved August 31, 2007, from Kuki International Forum Web site: http://www.kukiforum.com/kuki-people/history /130-leadership-in-the-military.html

Toner, C. (2006). Military service as a practice: Integrating the sword and shield approach to military ethics. *Journal of Military Ethics, 5*(3), 183-200. Retrieved June 24, 2009, from EBSCOhost database.

Toner, J. H. (2006). Educating for exemplary conduct. *Air and Space Power Journal, 20*(1), 18-26. Retrieved February 12, 2008, from EBSCOhost database.

Torr, J. D. (2005). U.S. policy toward rogue nations. *At Issue Series*. San Diego, CA: Greenhaven Press. Retrieved April 14, 2007, from Opposing Viewpoints database.

Trent Focus Group. (2002). *An introduction to qualitative research*. Retrieved June 9, 2009, from http://www.trentrdsu.org.uk/cms/uploads/Qualitative%20Research.pdf

Trochim, W. M. K. (2006). *Social research methods*. Retrieved March 24, 2008, from http://www.socialresearchmethods.net/kb/variable.php

Twair, P. M., & Powell, S. (2004). Protests around the world mark first anniversary of war on Iraq. *Washington Report on Middle East Affairs, 23*(4), 9. Retrieved July 30, 2009, from International Security and Counter Terrorism Reference Center database.

U.S. Historical Documents. (2008). *Franklin D. Roosevelt's infamy speech*. Retrieved October 12, 2008, from the University of Oklahoma College of Law Web site: http://www.law.ou.edu/ushistory/infamy.shtml

U.S. Marine Corps. (2008). *Values and ethics: Building the foundation of every Marine's character*. Retrieved October 25, 2008, from http://www.marines.com/main/ index/making_marines/recruit_training/training_matri/core_values_ethics

Ulysses S. Grant. (2006). *Grant, the world leader*. Retrieved September 9, 2007, from http://www.granthomepage.com/grantleader.htm

Underwood, M. (2003). Group leadership. *Interpersonal Communication: Leadership*. Retrieved August 30, 2007, from http://www.cultsock.ndirect.co.uk/MUHome/cshtml/groups/lead1.html

Van Eersel, F. M. (2008). *Managerial grid (Blake and Mouton)*. Retrieved October 11, 2008, from http://www.12manage.com/methods_blake_mouton_managerial _grid.html

Vandergriff, D. (2006). *Raising the bar: Creating and nurturing adaptability to deal with the changing face of war*. Washington, DC: Center for Defense Information Press.

Varughese, S. (2008). *Servant leadership: Stooping to conquer*. Retrieved April 1, 2008, from the Life Positive Web site: http://www.lifepositive.com/Mind/Ethics/ Servant_Leadership_stooping_to_conquer22004.asp

Velasquez, M., Andre, C., Shanks, T. S. J., & Meyer, M. J. (2008). What is ethics? Retrieved from the *Markkula Center for Applied Ethics* website: http://www.scu.edu/ethics/practicing/decision/whatisethics.html

Verweij, D., Hofhuis, K., & Soeters, J. (2007). Moral judgement [*sic*] within the armed forces. *Journal of Military Ethics, 6*(1), 19-40. Retrieved August 2, 2009, from International Security & Counter-Terrorism Reference Center database.

Warren, C. A. B., & Karner, T. X. (2005). *Discovering qualitative methods: Field research, interviews, and analysis*. Los Angeles: Roxbury.

Weinberg, L. B., Eubank, W. L., & Francis, E. A. (2008). The cost of terrorism: The relationship between international terrorism and democratic governance. *Terrorism and Political Violence, 20*(2), 257-270. Retrieved January 31, 2009, from ProQuest database.

Wester, E. (2007). *Last resort and preemption: Using armed force as a moral and penultimate choice*. Retrieved October 11, 2008, from http://www.carlisle. army.mil/usawc/Parameters/07summer/wester.pdf

Willenz, P. (2003, March 26). *Leadership styles that use rewards and shared values help platoons perform well in simulated combat conditions*. Retrieved August 31, 2007, from American Psychological Association Web site: http://www.apa.org /releases/leadership.html

Williams, D. C., & Levitt, H. M. (2007). A qualitative investigation of eminent therapists' values within psychotherapy: Developing integrative principles for moment-to-moment psychotherapy practice. *Journal of Psychotherapy Integration, 17*(2), 159-184. Retrieved September 7, 2008, from EBSCOhost database.

Williamson, A. (2005). *Biography of Joan of* Arc (Jeanne D'Arc). Retrieved May 20, 2007, from http://archive.joan-of-arc.org/joanofarc_short_biography.html

Wilson, B. A. (2005). *Women in combat: Why not?* Retrieved October 12, 2008, from http://userpages.aug.com/captbarb/combat.html

Wolpert, S. (2006). Alexander the Great. In *Encyclopedia of India* (Vol. 1). Detroit, MI: Scribner. Retrieved May 17, 2008, from Gale PowerSearch database.

Women rulers. (2007). Retrieved September 16, 2007, from the Women in World History Web site: http://www.womeninworldhistory.com/rulers.html

Wong, L. (2003). Military leadership: A context-specific review. *Leadership Quarterly, 14*(6), 657-692. Retrieved January 20, 2008, from ProQuest database.

Wren, D. A. (2005). *The history of management thought.* Hoboken, NJ: Wiley.

Yammarino, F. J., Dionne, S. D., Chun, J. U., & Dansereau, F. (2005). Leadership and levels of analysis: A state-of-the-science review. *The Leadership Quarterly, 16*(6), 879–919. Retrieved February 12, 2009, from ProQuest database.

Yeakey, G. W. (2002). Situational leadership. *Military Review.* Retrieved August 26, 2007, from the Air University Web site: http://www.au.af.mil/au/awc /awcgate/milreview/yeakey.htm

Yin, R. K. (2003). *Case study research: Design and method* (3rd ed.). Thousand Oaks, CA: Sage.

Yukl, G. (2010). *Leadership in organizations* (7th ed.). Upper Saddle River, NJ: Pearson Education.

APPENDIX A: PERMISSION TO USE PREMISES

UNIVERSITY OF PHOENIX

Permission to Use Premises, Name, and/or Subjects (Facility, Organization, University, Institution, or Association)

NAVAL BASE KITSAP

Name of Facility, Organization, University, Institution, or Association

Check any that apply:

☒ I hereby authorize Janice M. Brooks, student of University of Phoenix, to use the premises (facility identified below) to conduct a study entitled "The Values that Influence and Guide the Style and Practices of Successful Military Leaders."

☒ I hereby authorize Janice M. Brooks, student of University of Phoenix, to recruit subjects for participation in and conduct a study entitled "The Values that Influence and Guide the Style and Practices of Successful Military Leaders."

☒ I hereby authorize Janice M. Brooks, student of University of Phoenix, to use the name of the facility, organization, university, institution, or association identified above when publishing results from the study entitled "The Values that Influence and Guide the Style and Practices of Successful Military Leaders."

All authorizations are subject to the following conditions:

    1. Disclaimer - All statements made by any participants are those of the speaker and do not necessarily represent the views of Naval Base Kitsap, the U.S. Navy, or the Department of Defense.

    2. Use of organizational names, including "Naval Base Kitsap" and "U.S. Navy" shall be for identification purposes only and does not constitute an endorsement of any kind.

_____   ████████████

M. J. OLSON, Captain, U.S. Navy   Date
Naval Base Kitsap
Commanding Officer

Address of Facility:

Commanding Officer
Naval Base Kitsap
120 South Dewey Street
Bremerton, WA 98314-5020

APPENDIX B: PERMISSION TO USE PREMISIS

UNIVERSITY OF PHOENIX

PERMISSION TO USE PREMISES, NAME, AND/OR SUBJECTS
(Facility, Organization, University, Institution, or Association)

COMMANDER, SUBMARINE GROUP NINE

(Name of Facility, Organization, University, Institution, or Association)

Check any that apply:

☒ I hereby authorize Janice M. Brooks, student of University of Phoenix, to use the premises (facility identified below) to conduct a study entitled _The Values that Influence and Guide the Style and Practices of Successful Military Leaders._

☒ I hereby authorize Janice M. Brooks, student of University of Phoenix, to recruit subjects for participation in and conduct a study entitled _The Values that Influence and Guide the Style and Practices of Successful Military Leaders._

☒ I hereby authorize Janice M. Brooks, student of University of Phoenix, to use the name of the facility, organization, university, institution, or association identified above when publishing results from the study entitled _The Values that Influence and Guide the Style and Practices of Successful Military Leaders._

Rick Cutts   6 /18/10

Signature   Date

Rick L. Atkins

Name

CMDCM (ss)

Title,

Address of Facility

APPENDIX C: PERMISSION TO USE PREMISIS

UNIVERSITY OF PHOENIX

PERMISSION TO USE PREMISES, NAME, AND/OR SUBJECTS
(Facility, Organization, University, Institution, or Association)

<u>Fort Lewis (JBLM)</u>

(Name of Facility, Organization, University, Institution, or Association)

Check any that apply:

☒ I hereby authorize <u>Janice M. Brooks</u>, student of University of Phoenix, to use the premises (facility identified below) to conduct a study entitled *The Values that Influence and Guide the Style and Practices of Successful Military Leaders.*

☒ I hereby authorize <u>Janice M. Brooks</u>, student of University of Phoenix, to recruit subjects for participation in and conduct a study entitled *The Values that Influence and Guide the Style and Practices of Successful Military Leaders.*

☒ I hereby authorize <u>Janice M. Brooks</u>, student of University of Phoenix, to use the name of the facility, organization, university, institution, or association identified above when publishing results from the study entitled *The Values that Influence and Guide the Style and Practices of Successful Military Leaders.*

Signature *Matthew Barnes*

Date 11 May 2010

Name CSM Matthew D. Barnes

Title, Joint Base Garrison Command Sergeant Major

Address of Facility Mail Stop 1aa, Box 339500
Joint Base Lewis-McChord, WA 98433

APPENDIX D: PERMISSION TO USE PREMISIS

UNIVERSITY OF PHOENIX

PERMISSION TO USE PREMISES, NAME, AND/OR SUBJECTS
(Facility, Organization, University, Institution, or Association)

Provost Marshal Office, JBLM

(Name of Facility, Organization, University, Institution, or Association)

Check any that apply:

☒ I hereby authorize Janice M. Brooks, student of University of Phoenix, to use the premises (facility identified below) to conduct a study entitled _The Values that Influence and Guide the Style and Practices of Successful Military Leaders._

☒ I hereby authorize Janice M. Brooks, student of University of Phoenix, to recruit subjects for participation in and conduct a study entitled _The Values that Influence and Guide the Style and Practices of Successful Military Leaders._

☒ I hereby authorize Janice M. Brooks, student of University of Phoenix, to use the name of the facility, organization, university, institution, or association identified above when publishing results from the study entitled _The Values that Influence and Guide the Style and Practices of Successful Military Leaders._

Signature _[signature]_   Date 3/3/10

Name MYRON J. LEWIS

Title, PROVOST MARSHAL SGM

Address of Facility
Bldg 2007c , JBLM, WA 98433

APPENDIX E: MANDATED PRECEPTS FOR SMMC SELECTION BOARD

Excerpt is from CMC, Manpower Management Promotions Branch, *Precept for the board to select nominees to be considered as the 15th sergeant major of the Marine Corps.*

1. The board will recommend to CMC five sergeants major (with no priority assigned) whom the board considers "best qualified" (pg. 2) to serve in the billet of Sergeant Major of the Marine Corps. The board shall consider those sergeants major exhibiting proven excellence in war fighting skills, training and operational environments, and administrative capability. These individuals must be able to present the Marine Corps in many and varied forums, thus must be capable of clearly articulating Marine Corps interests and concerns.

2. The five nominees shall be selected from the pool of all Marines eligible to be considered as the SMMC.

3. The board shall carefully consider the personal appearance of each eligible Marine as evidenced by official photographs.

4. The board shall consider each marine's performance of assigned duties.

5. Particular effort is to be applied to the interpretation of the markings of fitness reports. In addition, the following shall be considered with respect to qualities, qualifications, attributes and professional conduct:

    a. Marines who have undergone the rigorous screening process, successfully completed the difficult training program, and performed difficult and demanding duties as a recruiter shall be considered "highly qualified" for nomination.

    b. Marines who successfully underwent the rigid screening process and rigorous training regimens and requirements of drill instructor duty shall be considered "highly qualified" for nomination.

c. A successful tour of duty under the stringent requirements and conditions imposed by the duties of a Marine Security Guard shall be considered indicative of superior leadership qualities. These marines shall be considered "highly qualified" for nomination.

d. Board members shall carefully consider the Marine Corps policy concerning alcoholism and alcohol abuse, and shall take into consideration any misconduct or reduction in performance resulting from such behavior.

e. Board members shall carefully consider the Marine Corps policy concerning the distribution, possession or use of illegal substances, and will consider such behavior in the evaluation of a Marine's potential.

6. A Marine's physical qualifications will also be carefully considered as revealed by the contents of official military medical documents.

7. Board members shall consider all documented incidents of misconduct and substandard performance which are included in a Marine's official record.

8. The board is also encouraged to be especially alert for sergeants major whose records indicate the embracement of change and innovation as evidenced by conceiving and trying new solutions to challenging problems. Bold creative thinkers who are calculated risk-takers, and who have shown initiative in the pursuit of highly effective means of accomplishing the Marine Corps mission is to be given priority in the nomination process.

9. The resulting board report shall certify that the board has carefully considered the records and accomplishments of all sergeants major whose names were submitted to the board, and that the majority opinion was used to recommend the best qualified sergeant major to serve as the Sergeant Major of the Marine Corps.

APPENDIX F: INFORMED CONSENT FORM

Dear_____,

I am a student at the University of Phoenix working on a Doctor of Management degree in Organizational Leadership. I am conducting a research study entitled Military Leadership: *The Values that Guide and Influence the Style and Practices of Successful Military Leaders*. The purpose of the proposed qualitative grounded theory research project is to explore the developed successful leadership styles and preferences of successful senior enlisted military leaders to determine the values by which they are informed. The study is intended to create and describe a model that will meet leadership training goals of developing a force committed to moral and ethical values while accomplishing the unique missions of a 21st century military force.

The purpose of this letter is to request your participation as a subject in the current study. Your participation will involve sharing information about your leadership style, preferences, and values in recorded interview sessions (in person or via telephone). Your participation is voluntary. If you choose not to participate or to withdraw from the study at any time, you can do so by providing a written statement to that effect without penalty or loss of benefit to yourself. The results of the research study may be published, however, as a subject your name will not be used in the study. In this research, there are no foreseeable risks to you.

Although there may be no direct benefit to you, the possible benefit of your participation is that you will be recognized, as a result of this project, as a valuable contributor to research advancing the disciplines of leadership and military leadership. If you agree to participate in this research study, please provide your informed consent by reading and signing the statement below.

If you have any questions concerning the research study during or after the study, you may contact me by calling 360-xxx-xxxx or 253-xxx-xxxx, or e-mail: semperfi98335@centurytel.net.

Sincerely,

_____

Janice M. Brooks

INFORMED CONSENT:

By signing this form, I acknowledge that I understand the nature of the study, any potential risks to me as a participant, and the means by which my identity will be kept confidential. My signature on this form also indicates that I am over the age of 18, I am not a member of any protected category of participants (minor, pregnant woman when considered part of a designated research group of women, prisoner, or cognitively impaired), and that I give my permission to voluntarily serve as a participant in the study described by Janice Brooks in the introduction to this letter.

_____

Name of Participant

_____   _____

Signature of Participant   Date

APPENDIX G: CONSENT FORM FOR SECONDARY PARTICIPANT

Dear_____,

I am a student at the University of Phoenix working on a Doctor of Management degree in Organizational Leadership. I am conducting a research study entitled Military Leadership: *The Values that Guide and Influence the Style and Practices of Successful Military Leaders.* The purpose of the proposed qualitative study is to explore the developed successful leadership styles and preferences of successful senior enlisted military leaders. The study is intended to create and describe a model that will meet leadership training goals of developing a force committed to moral and ethical values while accomplishing the unique missions of a 21st century military force.

The purpose of this letter is to request your participation in this qualitative grounded theory research study. As a subject in the study, your participation will involve sharing information about your experiences with one of the leaders whose leadership style and preferences you are familiar with by way of recorded interview sessions (in person or via telephone). Your participation is voluntary. If you choose not to participate or to withdraw from the study at any time, you can do so without penalty or loss of benefit to yourself. The results of the research study may be published and as the subject of this case study your name will not be used in the study without your express agreement.

In this research, there are no foreseeable risks to you. Although there may be no direct benefit to you, the possible benefit of your participation is that you will be recognized, as a result of this project, as a valuable contributor to research advancing the disciplines of leadership and military leadership. If you agree to participate in this research study, please provide your informed consent by reading and signing the statement below. If you have any questions concerning the research study, please call me at 360-xxx-xxxx or 253-xxx-xxxx.

Sincerely,

_____

Janice M. Brooks

INFORMED CONSENT:

By signing this form, I acknowledge that I understand the nature of the study, any potential risks to me as a participant, and the means by which my identity will be kept confidential. My signature on this form also indicates that I am over the age of 18, I am not a member of any protected category of participants (minor, pregnant woman when considered part of a designated research group of women, prisoner, or cognitively impaired), and that I give my permission to voluntarily serve as a participant in the study described by Janice Brooks in the introduction to this letter.

_____

Name of Participant

_____   _____

Signature of Participant   Date

APPENDIX H: PRETESTING
THE INTERVIEW STRUCTURE

Pre-testing the Interview Structure and Questions for Relevance and Clarity Pre-testing is an important process in the development of a research instrument (Cooper & Schindler 2006). The interviewing design and the preset open-ended interview questions will first be piloted, or pre-tested, for relevance and clarity by creating conditions that mimic those of the present study. The interview guide and questions as well as the interview format will be field-tested using small number of individuals as surrogates who agree to be subjected to the interview design and to respond to the interview questions. The researcher hopes to discover whether the research structure and the interview guide questions are appropriate for the research purpose as envisioned by the researcher. This appendix provides information on (a) testing the study instrument and protocol, (b) recruitment of participants, (c) conducting the pre-test interviews, and (d) pilot/pre-test discovery possibilities.

Testing the Study Instrument and Protocol
Four types of pre-testing procedures have been described by Cooper and Schindler (2006): they are researcher pre-testing, participant pre-testing, collaborative pre-testing, and non-collaborative pre-testing. The interview guide and format/protocol will be tested using participant pre-testing, which will consist of the same procedure as described for the present study. The pilot study will be conducted at a military installation with three or four unit leaders as participants. The pre-test participants will be individuals who have the same background and characteristics as the study participants. While they do not hold the same billets as the study participants, they will be military leaders of the most senior Staff Non-Commissioned Officer ranks (E-8 or E-9). The pilot design will be a replication of the present study protocol for the research and interview process. The surrogates will be informed of the purpose of the pilot study and asked to comment on the relevance

and clarity of the questions and the format as well. The pilot study participants will also be asked to sign an informed consent letter.

Recruitment of Participants

Participants must be 18 years of age or older, and hold a Staff Non-Commissioned Officer (SNCO) leadership billet with responsibility for guidance and training of subordinate troops.

Establishing access

The procedure for establishing access to pilot study participants will mirror the process for obtaining organizational approval to use premises, name, or subjects for the present study. Once approval is obtained from the local military installations from which the participants will be selected, pilot study participants will be identified and accessed by contacting the personnel administrative unit to inquire about possible volunteers. Recommendations for appropriate participants for the pilot study will be solicited from senior leaders. The leaders must demonstrate consent by executing the informed consent form.

Making contact with potential participants

From a list of 5–10 potential participants, each will be contacted via telephone (with follow-up e-mail) and asked if he or she might have an interest in participating in the pilot study. Three or four volunteers will be selected, based on any available recommendation by superiors. A briefing will be provided to potential participants who respond to the inquiry in order to explain the purpose of both the main research study and the pilot study. Three or four potential participants will then be invited to participate in the piloting process, and interview times will be established. After the pilot participants are identified, secondary or other pilot participants will be solicited from the primary pilot participants in order to test the relevance, clarity, and overall appropriateness of the questions and protocol for the secondary participant interviews. All study participants for the pilot study and actual study will be asked to sign an informed consent statement.

Conducting the Interviews

The interview guide will contain identical questions to those used on the present study. The interview process and structure will be the same as those identified in the study. The same procedures will be used for the secondary pre-test participants.

Pilot/Pre-Test Discovery Possibilities

Certain possible pre-test discoveries will be noted. Some common possibilities include those pertaining to (a) participant interest, (b) meaning, (c) transformation of questioning, (d) the flow and continuity of questions, (e) the sequence of the questions, (f) skipping and rerouting of questions, (g) variability of questions, (h) length and timing of the interviews, and (i) overall appropriateness of the research instrument/ interview guide (Cooper & Schindler 2006).

APPENDIX I: PRIMARY PARTICIPANTS INTERVIEW PROTOCOL

Leader/Interviewee: _____

Position: _____

Introduction:

Opening remarks: Thank you for taking the time to participate in this research study. The data collected from these interviews will used to fulfill the research project requirements of the University of Phoenix School of Advanced Studies, Doctor of Management Degree in Organizational Leadership. Data derived from these interviews will support the development of a theoretical leadership model describing the values that inform and influence successful military leaders. The interviews will be will be confidential, and will only be used only for the purpose described. You will neither be identified by name in the report nor in conversations with others. Two interview sessions (round one and round two), each approximately 90 minutes long or one session not to exceed 2 hours in length will be planned. *(Note: The interview time frame will be determined, based on the time and availability of the participants.)* Round one will consist of inquiries and discussions about personal leadership experience, and round two will consist of inquiries about leadership inspiration.

Explanation of the dissertation problem. World affairs in the 21st century coupled with an increased diversity in the nature of military missions has placed responsibilities on the United States military, demanding unparalleled leadership ethics, principles, methods, and practices for senior enlisted military members. Ultimately, the fallout of the problem rests with the young troops who without effective values-based leadership cannot be effective in carrying out their duties and responsibilities.

Explanation of the Study Purpose. Leading troops in the 21st century military environment requires more than skill, prowess technique, and tactics since the United States now confronts an unconventional adversary in the GWOT. The purpose of the study is to determine what personally and professionally-held values are causative to the leadership success of accomplished senior enlisted military personnel. The results of the study are intended to create and describe a model that will meet the leadership training goal of developing a military force committed to the moral values that are the foundation and strength of the American military and the American way of life. Based on your professional leadership experiences, qualities, and success, you have been asked to participate as a primary participant in the research study. Other secondary participants (i.e. peers, subordinates, mentors, family members, and lifetime acquaintances) whom you will be asked to identify will also be asked to provide insight into your leadership experiences.

Describe the interview Process. In this interview, you will be asked questions concerning your leadership style and experiences on a personal and professional basis, and your leadership inspiration and values. All responses will be tape recorded and will remain confidential with access limited to the researcher. The responses you provide will help the researcher gather information regarding the personal and professional values from which emanate your successful leadership, characteristics, styles and practices.

Round One

Personal Leadership Inquiries
Please respond to, and elaborate on the following questions as thoroughly as possible.

1. Please discuss your leadership experiences; both military and civilian.
   a. Describe your leadership experiences before joining the military.

    b. What military leadership roles have you held in the past? Please describe them.

    c. How many years of military leadership experience do you have?

2. Please discuss your personal theory on leadership and how you came to that theory.

3. Do you identify your leadership style with any particular category of leadership style? If so, which style do you identify with?

4. What traits and characteristics do you consider to be associated with your leadership style?

5. Has this style always been effective for you?

6. Please describe one or two circumstances in which you exhibited the traits and characteristics of this particular leadership style in successfully guiding, directing or influencing the actions of others to achieve goals and objectives.

7. Can your leadership style be effectively adapted to serve the needs of civilian leadership situations?

8. How significant, if at all, are personal and professional core values and beliefs to your leadership actions, decision-making practices and success as a military leader?

9. What proved more effective for you in leading troops? Legislated means such as rules, regulations, status, and laws, or your personal example and leadership style? How important, if at all, are personal virtues and morals to effective leadership?

10. What specific values, virtues, morals and ethical concepts guided your leadership actions and behavior?

11. Describe what you consider to be a successful culture conducive to an effective military learning, training and working environment?

12. What were your most successful motivational techniques in terms of calling your troops and followers to action in any given circumstance?

13. How important is the concept of ethics to military leadership?

14. What would you say are most significant deficiencies in today's military leadership? Why do you feel this is the case? What, in your opinion, can be done to correct this situation?

15. Please describe a typical day in your life as a military leader.

16. Given the GWOT and the unconventional warfare and battlefield situations faced by young troops today, are there any special training needs for troops and their leaders? If so, what would you propose for preparing military leaders for their task of training and leading troops today?

17. It has been said that leaders must eventually earn the true right to leadership from those being led. Do you agree? If so, how did you earn that right?

18. Please describe some specific attitudes, actions and practices you employed that helped you earn the loyalty, and respect of followers, peers, and superiors, and the recognition as a successful leader of military troops. How do these relate to your personal leadership theory?

19. What would you consider the biggest leadership challenge of your career? How did you face and meet the challenge?

20. What general advice would you offer leaders when faced with any type or magnitude of challenge?

21. In your opinion, how important is it, if at all, for leaders to "model the way" or set the example?

22. How important, if at all, is shared vision for a leader and followers? Describe your military leadership vision and its importance to you as a leader, and to your followers.

23. Have you ever found it necessary or worthwhile to challenge the normal process of things in your organization as pertains to the training and leadership of troops and followers? If so, explain why, and if possible provide an example of such a time.

24. What is your theory or opinion concerning the empowerment of followers to perform independently of orders or commands?

25. How important is a system of rewards, recognition, and encouragement to the development of followers?

26. Is there anything else you would like to share about your leadership values and their influence on your success as a leader?

Round 2

Leadership Inspiration Inquiries

1. Identify the person (or persons), military or otherwise who you feel most influenced and inspired your development as an individual, as a Marine, and as a military leader. Why? What characteristics or traits did you admire most in these people? What was the most important thing you learned from each?
2 Who influenced and inspired you as an individual?
    a. Why?
    b. What are their most admired characteristics?
    c. What are the most important lesson learned from this person?
3. Who influenced and inspired you as a young soldier/sailor/marine/airman?
    a. Why?
    b. What are their most admired characteristics?
    c. What are the most important lesson learned from this person?
4. Who influenced and inspired you as a military leader?
    a. Why?
    b. What are their most admired characteristics?
    c. What are the most important lesson learned from this person?
5. Identify a personality (historical or present) whom you may not necessarily have been inspired or influenced by, but whom you admire for his or her leadership success and effectiveness. Explain why.

APPENDIX J: SECONDARY PARTICIPANTS INTERVIEW PROTOCOL

Leader/Participant: _____

Interviewee # _____

Relationship to leader: _____

Title or Position: _____

Introduction:

Opening remarks: Thank you for taking the time to participate in this research study. One interview session, approximately 90 minutes long, is planned. As discussed previously, the data collected from these interviews will used to fulfill the research project requirements of the University of Phoenix School of Advanced Studies, Doctor of Management Degree in Organizational Leadership. Data derived from these interviews will support the development of a theoretical leadership model describing the values that inform and influence successful military leaders. The interviews will be confidential and will only be used only for the purpose described. You will not be identified by name either in the report or in conversations with others.

Explanation of the dissertation problem. World affairs in the 21st century coupled with an increased diversity in the nature of military missions has placed responsibilities on the United States military demanding unparalleled leadership ethics, principles, methods, and practices for senior enlisted military members. Ultimately, the fallout of the problem rests with the young troops who without effective values-based leadership cannot be effective in carrying out their duties and responsibilities.

Explain the Study Purpose. Leading troops in the 21st century military environment requires more than skill, prowess technique, and tactics since the United States now confronts an unconventional adversary in the current GWOT. The purpose of the study is to determine what personally and professionally-held values are causative to the leadership success of accomplished senior enlisted military personnel. The results of the study are intended to create and describe a model that will meet the leadership training goal of developing a military force committed to the moral values that are the foundation and strength of the American military and the American way of life. Based on your personal and professional acquaintance with the subject, you are being asked to participate in this interview.

Describe the interview Process. In this interview, you will be asked questions concerning the leadership style and experiences of one of the primary participants in the study. You are asked to answer all questions as candidly and as thoroughly as possible. All responses will be tape recorded, but will remain confidential with access limited to the researcher. The responses you provide will help the researcher gather information regarding the personal and professional values that contribute to the subject's successful leadership styles, characteristics, and practices.

Please respond to, and elaborate on the following questions:

1. How long have you known the subject, and under what conditions were you first acquainted with him/her?
2. Please describe your personal or professional relationship with the subject?
3. How would you characterize the subject's leadership style?
4. In your opinion, is his style effective? If so, what do you feel accounts for the success and effectiveness of his style? Please explain using examples and illustrations.
5. What do you consider the most impressive attribute the subject demonstrates?
6. Discuss the work ethic, integrity, and values of the subject. How do these concepts impact the success of this leader?
7. Have you known or observed this leader in the role of follower? If so, please explain.

8. What other, if any, relevant information would you like to share concerning the subject that may contribute to this case study.
9. Identify and explain some of the specific values you feel influence the style and practices of this leader.
10. Describe your most memorable experience with this leader.

APPENDIX K: PERMISSION TO INCLUDE CONTENT

Legal/Permissions
One Lake Street
Upper Saddle River, NJ 07458
Fax: 201-236-3290
Phone: 201-236-3275
Barbara.Wood@Pearson.com

Nov 30, 2009   PE Ref # 149761

JANICE M. BROOKS
3717 26th. Ave. Ct., NW
Gig Harbor, WA 98335

Dear Madam:

You have our permission to include content from our text, *LEADERSHIP IN ORGANIZATIONS*, *7th Ed. by YUKL, GARY,* in your dissertation or masters thesis for your course at University of Phoenix.

Content to be included is:
88 Fig. 4-1

Please credit our material as follows:
YUKL, GARY, LEADERSHIP IN ORGANIZATIONS, 7th Edition, © 2010. Reprinted by permission of Pearson Education, Inc., Upper Saddle River, NJ

Sincerely,

Barbara Wood, Permissions Administrator

APPENDIX L: RESEARCH QUESTION ANSWER GUIDE

Research Question (RQ)	Protocol Question Summary (Potential RQ Answers) R = Round PQ = Protocol Question
RQ1 – Values (Yellow)	R1PQ4 – Traits and Characteristics R1PQ9 – Troop leading practices and measures R1PQ10 – Guiding values, morals, ethical concepts R1PQ11 – Elements of a successful military cultures R1PQ15 – Typical daily actions and activities R1PQ20 – Dealing with challenges R1PQ25 – Significance of reward systems R2PQ1 – Inspirational influences (admired characteristics) R2PQ2 – Admired personalities
RQ2 – Actions, Practices, Behaviors (Green)	R1PQ6 – Guiding, directing and influencing the actions of others R1PQ9 – Troop leading practices and measures R1PQ15 – Typical daily actions and activities R1PQ17 – Earning the right to lead R1PQ18 – Attitudes, practices, behaviors R1PQ19 – Leadership challenges R1PQ21 – Modeling the way/setting the example R1PQ24 – Empowerment of followers R1PQ25 – Significance of reward systems R2PQ2 – Admired personalities
RQ3 – Facing Leadership Challenges (Pink)	R1PQ12 – Successful motivational techniques R1PQ15 – Typical daily actions and activities R1PQ16 – Special GWOT training needs for troops and leaders R1PQ19 – Leadership challenges R1PQ21 – Modeling the way/setting the example R1PQ22 – Importance of shared vision R1PQ23 – Challenging the status quo of organizational leadership R2PQ2 – Admired personalities

Table continued

Research Question (RQ)	Protocol Question Summary (Potential RQ Answers) R = Round PQ = Protocol Question
RQ4 – Successful Leadership Models, Theories, Styles (Blue	R1PQ2 – Personal leadership theory
	R1PQ3 – Participant leadership style
	R1PQ5 – Effectiveness of participant's style
	R1PQ7 – Adaptibility of participant's leadership style
	R1PQ15 – Typical daily actions and activities
	R1PQ19 – Leadership challenges
	R1PQ20 – Dealing with challenges
	R1PQ21 – Modeling the way/setting the example
	R1PQ22 – Importance of shared vision
	R1PQ24 – Empowerment of followers
	R1PQ25 – Significance of reward systems
	R2PQ1 – Inspirational influences (admired characteristics)
	R2PQ2 – Admired personalities